Three Mirrors
for Two Biblical Ladies
Susanna and the Queen of Sheba
in the Eyes of
Jews, Christians, and Muslims

Three Mirrors for Two Biblical Ladies Susanna and the Queen of Sheba in the Eyes of Jews, Christians, and Muslims

FABRIZIO A. PENNACCHIETTI

GORGIAS PRESS
2006

First Gorgias Press Edition, 2006.

ISBN 1-59333-319-6

GORGIAS PRESS
46 Orris Ave., Piscataway, NJ 08854 USA
www.gorgiaspress.com

Printed and bound in the United States of America.

CONTENTS

Foreword

In the Old Testament's gallery of female portraits, two figures stand out with particular splendour: the Queen of Sheba, a sovereign of a remote kingdom, and the noble Susanna, "a God-fearing woman of rare beauty". The first of these is represented as an exceptional woman who directly exercises royal power and pursues an ideal of knowledge and wisdom; the second is also said to have been a queen, for an ancient Jewish tradition identifies her as the wife of Jehoiachin and sister of Zerubbabel, the penultimate and the last king of Judah respectively. Devout thinkers have hazarded allegorical interpretations that have fired the imagination of secular narrators with regard to these two biblical ladies in every age of the written or oral literature of peoples of Jewish, Christian or Islamic faith. As familiar in Asia as in Africa and in Europe, Susanna and the Queen of Sheba have not failed to inspire the most famous painters and the most renowned musicians of the Western world.

If Susanna and the Queen of Sheba had really existed – which seems unlikely – and had learned how their image would be interpreted and described by future generations, they would certainly have been astonished, perhaps amused and even – why not? – indignant. But as figments of the imagination they are entirely unaware of the intermediate place they occupy in the development of still older legends. In point of fact, behind Susanna can be discerned the myth of the Dioscuri, the Heavenly Twins who became infatuated with a mortal woman, and the corresponding apocalyptic myth of two lustful fallen angels; on the other hand, behind the Queen of Sheba legends still survive on the miraculous powers of Solomon as a builder and a healer. The bustle of the devils whom he subdues with his seal ring but who still conspire against the Queen is duly soft-pedalled.

This volume offers an account of the series of transformations undergone by the tales of the two biblical ladies across time and space.

SUSANNA IN THE DESERT: REFLECTIONS OF A BIBLE STORY IN ARAB-ISLAMIC CULTURE[1]

1 Introduction

In the first few centuries of Arab-Islamic literature it is no easy matter to distinguish religious from profane tales. Arab culture in the high Middle Ages was radically imbued with the principles of the new religion; hence the borderline between the edifying and the escapist in narrative is even less clear than in medieval European culture.[2]

An obvious example of the fusion of religious and profane narrative motifs, as well as the mingling of registers typical of the miraculous with those characteristic of the wonderful, can be found in an unpublished Arabic manuscript entitled *The story of the skull and the king*. The name of the author and the period when the tale was composed are alike unknown. There are, however,

---

[1] The Italian original version has been published as a booklet in 1998 (*Susanna nel deserto. Riflessi di un racconto biblico nella cultura arabo-islamica*, Turin: Silvio Zamorani).

[2] Cf. Dalcorno *Modelli agiografici.* In ancient Arab literature, apart from those texts dealing with the biography of the Prophet, religious narrative consists of edifying stories about the prophets prior to Mohammed, the so-called *qiṣaṣ al-anbiyā'* "Stories of the Prophets", cf. the entry for *Ḳiṣaṣ al-anbiyā'* by T. Nagel in *E.I.*[2], V, 1986, 177-178. The oldest manuscript on the adventures of an "Islamic prophet" is the *Story of King David*, a papyrus codex dated 844, cf. Khoury *Wahb b. Munabbih*, I, 33-115. On the contrary secular Arab narrative is represented by tales of wonders, intended for nocturnal entertainment, such as the *Thousand and One Nights*. The oldest fragment of this literary genre – MS. No. 17618 of the Oriental Institute of the University of Chicago – has been dated to the first quarter of the 9th century, which corresponds in the West to the period of the first Carolingians, cf. Khoury *Mille et Une Nuits*, 32-33.

various indications which suggest that it is a work of antiquity, since it directly reflects the literary spirit of the first generations of Islam, of those storytellers who were able to edify while they entertained, and to reconcile prose with poetry.[1]

At the centre of the tale is Susanna, a figure almost completely unfamiliar in Islamic culture. In the West her story has seduced famous artists;[2] in Islamic culture, her name does not inspire emotion of any kind. She is mentioned neither in the Koran nor in the *Stories of the Prophets* (*Qiṣaṣ al-anbiyā'*);[3] the only Arab texts known thus far in which she figures are, as we shall see, a brief exemplum cited in the 16th century by Dāwud al-Antākī (§ 2.1), and an anecdote included in some Egyptian editions of the *Thousand and One Nights* (§ 2.2). In contrast, Susanna is given considerable space in the *Story of the skull and the king*, though the Bible story is reshaped along new lines, in a narrative frame whose models it would be interesting to trace.

1.1 *The tale of 'Susanna and the elders' in the Book of Daniel*

The tale of 'Susanna and the elders' is entirely marginal within the Old Testament: it is one of the four sections added to the *Book of Daniel*, in this case Chapter 13: the other three are the *Prayer of Azariah*, the canticle of the three young men in the fiery furnace (*Daniel* 3:24-90) and the story of *Bel and the dragon* (*Daniel* 14). As a supplementary text, *Susanna* was excluded from the list of normative texts when the canon of the Hebrew Bible

---

[1] On the characteristics of the earliest Islamic narrative literature, see Khoury *Mille et Une Nuits,* 25-29.

[2] The reproduction of important paintings from all periods showing the episode (from the so-called Lothair's Crystal, 9th century, to Delacroix, 19th century) illustrates Ornella Casazza's essay on the iconographic history of Susanna. This essay has been published as an appendix to the volume edited by Paolo Orvieto: Lucrezia Tornabuoni, *La istoria della casta Susanna*, Bergamo 1992: Moretti e Vitali editori. Lucrezia Tornabuoni (1425-1482), mother of Lorenzo the Magnificent, dedicated a laud of 135 tercets to Susanna.

[3] See above, note 2, p. 7. The most recent and thorough treatment of the stories of the prophets of Islam is the doctoral thesis by Roberto Tottoli, *Le* Qiṣaṣ al-anbiyā' *di Ṭarafī*, Napoli 1996 (Istituto Universitario Orientale di Napoli. Dipartimento di Studi e Ricerche su Africa e Paesi Arabi).

was fixed. As a result the original, in a Semitic language, probably Aramaic, was not copied, and hence was lost.[1] The tale of Susanna is, however, an integral part of the ancient Greek version of the Septuagint[2] and of all those versions of the Bible deriving from it, whether directly or by way of Theodotion's Greek revision.[3] In any case, Hebrew culture never forgot the episode, and it has been rooted in the Jewish folklore of all ages.[4] Well-known as the story is, it may be convenient to summarise it at this point:

> Susanna, daughter of Hilkiah, a pious and unusually lovely woman, mother of four children,[5] was the wife of a wealthy man named Joakim, who had been deported along with other Hebrews to Babylon. Joakim had a large house surrounded by a park to which, every morning, two judges were allowed admission to hear cases: these men were 'elders of the people'. They became infatuated with Susanna, and when they discovered that they were both in the grip of the same passion they conspired to rape her.[6] They slipped into the park unseen and caught Susanna alone,

---

[1] J.T. Milik, *Susanne à Qumrān*, 355-357, however, claims to have identified three tiny fragments of Qumran (4Q551), written in Aramaic in the second half of the 1st century BC, which may be connected with Susanna.

[2] On the Greek Septuagint version of the tale of Susanna, see Geissen *Susanna, Bel et Draco*; Moore *Daniel*, 77-116, and Engel *Die Susanna-Erzählung*.

[3] The episode is usually placed, as in the Septuagint, after Chapter 12 of the *Book of Daniel*, whereas in the Greek recension made by Theodotion (2nd century AD) and in the *Vetus Latina* it precedes Chapter 1. For the Catholic Church the tale of Susanna became an established part of the canon (though deuterocanonical) with the Council of Trent in 1546; the Greek Church, with the Jerusalem Synod of 1677, simply considers it an ecclesiastic text, excluded from the canon, while the Reformed Churches regard it as apocryphal.

[4] For a bibliography on the fortunes of the tale of Susanna in Jewish folklore, see Wurmbrand *Falasha Susanna* and Schwarzbaum *Prolegomenon*, 73-74. A collateral variant of the tale can be found in the Babylonian Talmud, *Sanhedrin* fol. 93a, translated by Gaster in *Jerahmeel*, Ch. LXIV, 200-202: "The Midrash of Ahab ben Qolaya and Zedekiah ben Ma'aseyah". Two false prophets, cited in *Jeremiah* 29:21-23, try to seduce the daughter of Nebuchadnezzar.

[5] Only the Greek text of the Septuagint says that Susanna was at the time the mother of four children.

[6] In order to seduce her (v. 22) according to Theodotion's recension.

waiting for her maids to bring her perfumes and oils for her bath. Hastening towards her, they began to threaten her that if she did not yield to their lust, they would announce publicly that they had caught her *in flagrante* with an unknown young man. When she resisted, they slandered her before the people and had her condemned to death by stoning. At this point the angel of the Lord[1] inspired the prophet Daniel, then a young man. He stepped forward, claiming that the accused had been condemned without a proper investigation, and asked to interrogate the two authoritative 'witnesses' himself, separately. When the assembly consented, Daniel asked each of them to say which tree Susanna had been lying under with the young man, and in what part of the park.[2] One said 'Under a mastic tree', the other, 'Under an ilex.' Having brought out the discordancy between their replies, Daniel declared them guilty and prophesied that they would be punished by the angel of the Lord. As a result, the assembly cleared Susanna and condemned the two false witnesses to death. According to the Septuagint they were tied up, taken outside the city and thrown into a ravine, whereupon the angel of the Lord hurled a lightning bolt at them. Theodotion says merely that the death penalty was applied in accordance with the Law of Moses.

1.2 *Antecedents of the tale of Susanna in folklore and mythology*

In the past twenty years scholars have concentrated their attention on two problems posed by the text of *Susanna*: its functional character within the sacred text, and its possible sources.[3]

---

[1] Only the Septuagint version relates the intervention of the Angel of the Lord who granted the youth the spirit of discernment.

[2] The twofold question appears only in the Septuagint version, because in Theodotion's recension the cross-examination is entirely concerned with what kind of tree it was. In both versions, however, it is only the answer to the first question that is reported. Milik, *Susanne à Qumrān*, 350-351, assumes that in the original Aramaic text the answer to the twofold question gave way to an alliterative pun such as *tḥt 'rb' b-m'rb'* "Under the poplar in the western part" and *tḥt ṣpṣpt' b-ṣpwn* "Under the willow in the northern part". The suggestion is that the translator made no attempt to render the Semitic *calembour* in Greek.

[3] I refer to the state of the matter expounded by Alessandro Catastini in 1988 in a brilliant article: "Il racconto di Susanna: riconsiderazioni di ipotesi vecchie e nuove" (Catastini *Susanna*, 195-196).

Discussion of possible reasons for its insertion in the *Book of Daniel* reveals two conflicting ideas:

1) For some, *Susanna* is a didactic tale whose aims are essentially moral and religious.[1] This hypothesis has recently been raised again by H. Engel, who maintains that Susanna represents the people of Judah, innocent and under threat, while the two wicked judges are their enemies.[2]

2) For others, from N. Brüll[3] in an article published in 1877 to A. Catastini in 1988,[4] the tale of Susanna has a precise, concrete aim, though within the didactic genre. These scholars see it as a polemical, satirical libel for anti-Sadducean ends, supposedly put together from a reworking of an old popular legend by a supporter of the Pharisee leader Simeon ben Shetach. According to this hypothesis, *Susanna* would therefore have been written in the last few years of the reign of Alexander Janneus, between 90 and 85 BC, in the context of the struggle between the Pharisees and the Sadducees for supremacy in the Gerousia, the council of the elders of the people.[5]

In this case, the two judges who abuse their own authority to extort a sexual favour would represent the arrogance of the aristocratic power of the Sadducees, while the young Daniel would be the emerging class of the Pharisees, eager to reform the judiciary procedures in force under their adversaries.

As to the problem of identification of the sources drawn on by the unknown author of *Susanna*, on the basis of Catastini's article the following three hypotheses can be recorded:[6]

---

[1] Cf. Catastini *Susanna*, 195 and note 9, 202. The relevant bibliography is in Pfeiffer *History of the New Testament Times*, 450; Busto Saiz *Interpretación del relato de Susanna*, 12-30.

[2] Cf. Catastini *op. cit.*, 195 and note 10, 202; Engel *Die Susanna-Erzählung*, 178-179.

[3] Brüll *Susanna-Buch*, 1-69.

[4] Catastini *op. cit.*, 196-201.

[5] This struggle ended at the beginning of the reign of Salome Alexandra with the abolition of the aristocratic Council of the Elders and the creation of the Synedrium, in which the Pharisees were at last in the majority, cf. *Dictionary of the Bible*, IV, 467-468. On this occasion there was a heated argument between the Pharisees and the Sadducees about the criteria for conducting trials for offences punishable by death.

[6] Catastini *op. cit.*, 195.

A) It may be a Judaic legend known in another form to Origen [1] and St. Jerome; [2] this legend is said to have been prompted by a Haggadic interpretation of *Jer.* 29:21-23, which speaks of the two false prophets Ahab and Zedekiah who were guilty of adultery, a detail which supplies the prompt for a link with the two false witnesses, the 'elders' (πρεσβύτεροι), who want to lead Susanna into carnal sin and, when she refuses, take their revenge by carrying out their threat to accuse her unjustly.[3]

B) Others believe that they can recognise in *Susanna* the themes of a myth to be sought in Babylonian and Greek sources; they see features in the heroine of a goddess of love and virginity, or of a sun goddess.[4]

C) For many, the most convincing hypothesis is that of the folk tale in a broad sense. In this case, the story of Susanna may be seen as a product of a fable genre of pure fiction, whose themes can be recognised in those of the 'wise young man' (the role played in this case by Daniel) and of 'Geneviève' (the lovely woman falsely accused). This hypothesis has found considerable support among the most recent studies.[5]

I personally hold that there is a useful combination to be made between the data inferred from the comparative study of popular tales from a typological standpoint, and the specific data of research into folklore and mythology. Indeed, I am convinced that the primitive nucleus, or rather the warp, of the tale of 'Susanna and the elders' consists essentially of the attempted seduction of a young woman by two persons of authority, the woof being the interweaving of the narrative themes of the 'lovely slandered woman' and the 'wise young man'.

---

[1] Catastini *op. cit.*, note 3, 201: Origenes, *Epistola ad Africanum de Susannae historia*, in J.-P. Migne, *Patrologia Graeca* 11, 63-66.

[2] Catastini *op. cit.*, note 4, 201: St. Jerome, *Commentaria in Jeremiam prophetam*, in J.-P. Migne, *Patrologia Latina* 24, 896-897.

[3] Catastini *op. cit.*, note 5, 202: Fritzsche-Grimm *Kurzgefasstes exegetisches Handbuch*, 84-85; Delcor *Le livre de Daniel*, 278. The episode of Ahab and Zedekiah is narrated in the Babylonian Talmud, *Sanhedrin* fol. 93a; see above, note 4, p. 9.

[4] Catastini *op. cit.*, note 6, 202; see the bibliography in Pfeiffer *History of New Testament Times*, 452-453.

[5] Catastini *op. cit.*, 195-196 and note 8, 202: Thompson *Motif-Index*, IV, 76-81, 480-482.

In Jewish tradition, the story which most closely reflects what I believe to have been the original plot of *Susanna* is the medieval *midrash* of Shemḥazay and ‘Aza’el, an exegetical tale which seems to be an ɧtiological legend of two exceedingly heterogeneous orders of things: on the one hand, one of the stars of the Pleiades, on the other the interjections of exhaustion and pain.

1.2.1 *The* midrash *of Shemḥazay and ‘Aza’el*[1]

This *midrash*, from the 11th century at latest, is a condensed version of part of the contents of the *Book of Giants*, a Judaic work of uncertain date, from the period between the third and first centuries BC.[2] Briefly, the story is as follows:

> Shemḥazay and ‘Aza’el[3] were two angels who had asked the Lord’s permission to live among humans. When they arrived on earth they were attracted by the daughters of men. Shemḥazay,[4] specifically, fell desperately in love with a girl named Estera[5] and tried to seduce her. To gain time, Estera promised to let him have his way with her, if he would tell her the Inexpressible name which permitted him to ascend into heaven. As soon as Shemḥazay uttered this name, Estera repeated it, thus immediately freeing herself from the harassment of the angel. The Lord rewarded her virtue and initiative by turning her into one of the Pleiades. Shemḥazay and ‘Aza’el had children by other women. One night, Shemḥazay’s two sons, Heyya and Aheyya, had a strange dream which they asked their father to interpret. On the basis of a prophecy by the patriarch Enoch, he told them that they would both die in the flood, but that by way of compensation their

---

[1] Cf. Milik *Books of Enoch*, 321-333; Gaster *Jerahmeel*, Ch. XXV, 52-54 (“The Midrash of Shemhazai and Azael”); Ginzberg *Legends*, 1, 147-151: “the Punishment of the Fallen Angels”.

[2] In Qumran a few fragments were found of the *Book of the Giants*, in Aramaic; this book was part of the so-called *Enochian Pentateuch*, cf. Milik *op. cit.*, 298-339.

[3] The name Shemḥazay appears in the forms *šmḥz’y*, *šmḥzy*, *šmḥwzy*, *šmyḥzh* and *šmyḥz’* “my Name has seen”; as for ‘Aza’el there are also the variants ‘Azaz’el and ‘Asa’el “God has done”, cf. Milik *op. cit.*, 428 and 437.

[4] Variants: Esṭērah, Isṭērah and Isṭehar, cf. Milik *op. cit.*, 323.

[5] *Book of Jubilees*, Ch. IV, 15, cf. Sacchi *Apocrifi*, 236; Milik *op. cit.*, 29.

names would be spoken in future every time anyone grunted as he lifted a heavy weight. Shemḥazay repented of his sin and from then on was suspended upside down between heaven and earth, while 'Aza'el continued undaunted to seduce men and women.

The male characters in this story are well known: Shemḥazay and 'Aza'el are the main exponents of the angelic category of Watchers, angels of the Lord who, according to the *Book of Jubilees*, an apocalyptic Jewish work of the 2nd century BC, came down among humans to instruct them and to impose justice on the earth.[1] At the same time, according to a tradition reflected by the *Book of Watchers* (4th-3rd century BC), the *Book of Parables* (end of 1st century BC) and Qumranic fragments in Aramaic from the *Book of Giants* – all three works belonging to the apocalyptic cycle of the patriarch Enoch – they are the two leaders of the host of rebel angels[2] whose union with the daughters of men was the origin of the race of Giants.[3] The two giants Heyya and Aheyya are also well known: they too are mentioned in the Qumranic fragments,[4] and also in Greek, Middle-Persian and Sogdian fragments of the Manichaean *Book of Giants.*

The name of the heroine, Estera, is on the other hand entirely new, and since it seems to be of Iranian origin, it raises a fascinating question. Estera is actually the transcription of a name which, in Persian, means both 'celestial body' and 'the planet Venus' (*setāre*).[5] This second meaning seems to link the heroine

---

[1] Cf. Ethiopian Enoch: *Book of the Watchers*, vi,3; vi,7; ix,6-8; *Book of Parables*, lxix,2, in, respectively, Sacchi *Apocrifi*, *Book of Enoch*, 472-473, 476 and 564; fragments 7 and 8 of the Dead Sea text *4QGiants*[a], García Martínez *Testi di Qumran*, 428-429. According to the *Book of Watchers*, vi, 5, the angels who swore and committed each other to form unions with the daughters of men were two hundred in number. In the fragments of the Manichaean *Book of the Giants*, written in Middle Persian in the 3rd century AD, Shemḥazay takes the form *šhmyz'd* "Shahmīzād", cf. Henning *Book of the Giants*, 54, 60.

[2] Cf. *Genesis* 6:21. The Watcher 'Aza'el is mentioned as 'Azaz'el in *Leviticus* 16:8, 10, 26, cf. Deiana *Azazel in Leviticus 16.*

[3] *4QGiants*[a], fr. 4 and 7; *4QGiants*[b]; *4QGiants*[c], fr. 2, cf. García Martínez *op. cit.*, 428, 430, 431.

[4] Cf. Henning *op. cit.*, 53-54, 65-66, 69-70; García Martínez *Qumran and Apocalyptic*, 106-107.

[5] Cf. Grünbaum *Vergleichende Mythologie*, 227-228; Milik *op. cit.*, 330-331; Steingass *Persian-English Dictionary*, 654.

of the *midrash* of Shemḥazay and ʻAza'el with the heroine of a parallel Islamic legend of obviously Iranian origin. In the various versions of this ancient legend, the female character becomes, not one of the Pleiades, but the planet Venus, whose name she bears in the forms Zuhara (Arabic: splendour), Bīdokht (Persian: childless woman) and Nāhid or Nāhīd (Arabo-Persian: woman with swollen breasts).[1]

1.2.2 *The Islamic legend of Hārūt and Mārūt*

Here is a summary of the Islamic legend of the fallen angels Hārūt and Mārūt as expounded by Georges Dumézil in his posthumous collection of essays, *Le roman des jumeaux*.[2]

> Hārūt and Mārūt were two angels who moved freely between heaven and earth. One day, they were approached for help by a young married woman who was on bad terms with her husband. The two angels were inflamed with passion for her and tried to steal her from her husband. In order to confuse them, the young woman offered them wine and then, pretending to yield to them, suggested that they tell her the secret word which made it possible for them to ascend into heaven. In their inebriated state the angels assented, and she was thus able immediately to go up to heaven, where God turned her into the planet Venus. The angels were punished by being reduced to the status of devils and were hung

[1] Cf. Grünbaum *op. cit.*, 227-228. In point of fact, the name Nāhid or Nāhīd is a transcription of Anahita ("the immaculate woman"), the Zoroastrian goddess who presides at the legendary spring Ardvi Sura, from which all the waters of the earth flow; she is at the same time the goddess who is manifested in the planet Venus, held to be a watery planet, cf. Ringbom *Paradisus*, 75-83.

[2] "La déchéance des anges Hārūt et Mārūt" in Dumézil *Roman des jumeaux* 67-78. There are various versions of the Islamic legend, according to the commentators on the Koran, cf. the entry "Hārūt wa-Mārūt" in *E.I.*^{2}, III, 1971, 243-244, by G. Vajda. The theologian Ibn Kathīr (d. 1372) attributed the legend to Kaʻb al-Aḥbār, a Yemenite scholar who converted to Islam at the time of the Prophet (Ibn Kathīr, *al-Bidāya wa-n-nihāya*, 3rd edit., Beirut 1979: Maktabat al-Maʻārif, I, 37-38, 48, lines 10-14). As his sources Dumézil (*op. cit.*, 67-68) quotes Grünbaum *op. cit.*, 225-229 and 322-323, note 45; and de Menasce *Légende indo-iranienne*.

up by the feet in a well in Babylon, where they taught men the occult arts.[1]

It must be assumed that this legend was circulating in pre-Islamic times, since the Koran mentions the fallen angels Hārūt and Mārūt in clear words, when it says that it was from them that men learned 'charms to separate a man from his woman'.[2]

Although, unlike the *midrash* of Shemḥazay and 'Aza'el, this legend does not include the narrative themes of the 'lovely slandered woman' (the so-called motif of 'Geneviève') and the wise young man who comes to her aid – two of the constituents of the story of Susanna – it nevertheless stands out by virtue of two details which bring it closer to the biblical story than the midrashic tale.

In the first place, the heroine of the Islamic legend is not a young unmarried woman as in the *midrash*, but an attractive married woman as in *Susanna*. Secondly, the male characters who abuse their power in making an attempt on a spouse's chastity, are two in number, like the powerful judges who try to seduce Susanna, whereas in the Jewish exegetic tale this is attributed solely to Shemḥazay. This latter detail is important because the Islamic legend seems to reflect the narrative archetype from which both tales derive more closely than the *midrash*. It is known that the exotic names Hārūt and Mārūt represent the Neo-Persian and then Arabic forms of the Avestan names Haurvatāt and Ameretāt.[3] These are the names of two of the 'Immortal Saints' (*Amesha Spenta*) whom Dumézil identifies with the 'Archangels' of Zoroastrianism.[4] As patrons respectively of water and of plants, Haurvatāt and Ameretāt had the function, according to the Avesta, of procuring health for human beings and freeing them from death.[5]

---

[1] On the presence of Hārūt and Mārūt in Daniel's well in Babylon, as we are told by Arabian writers such as al-Mas'ūdī, Yāqūt, al-Ḥimyarī and al-Qazwīnī, see Janssen *Bābil, the City of Witchcraft*, 187-193.

[2] Cf. *Koran* ii, 102.

[3] Cf. Grünbaum *op. cit.*, 225-229 and 322-323, note 45; Dumézil *op. cit.*, p. 67.

[4] Dumézil *op. cit.*, 60.

[5] Cf. Dumézil *op. cit.*, 59-66; Duchesne-Guillemin *Ancient Iran*, 336. As they are abstract but effective entities, the name Haurvatāt means

We owe to Dumézil the identification in Haurvatāt and Ameretāt of the Zoroastrian 'deformation' of the Heavenly Twins, so dear to classical and, in general, Indo-European mythology. From time immemorial the 'Twin Knights'[1] have been regarded by the Indo-European peoples as lower-order divinities, especially close to humans, on whom they bestowed favours according to the needs of the moment: nourishment, healing, protection from danger, happy marriages.[2]

However, Dumézil has also traced an archetype common to both the parallel Judaic and Islamic legends and to the story of Susanna.[3] This archetype has been identified in a specific episode of the Vedic version of the myth of Castor and Pollux, in which it emerges that the Heavenly Twins were attracted by a beautiful married woman.

1.2.3 *The Indo-European myth of Sukanyā and the Heavenly Twins*

The mythological incident which I have outlined here must have been enormously popular, if it is true that it is alluded to in bas-reliefs on ancient archaeological remains, such as the gold vase of Hasanlu,[4] Iranian Azerbaijan, of the 12th-11th century BC,

---

'health', while Ameretāt means 'immortality'.

[1] In Sanskrit the Heavenly Twins are called *Asvinau* "the two Knights, the two Charioteers", or *Nāsatyau* (cf. Monier-Williams *Sanskrit Dictionary*, 116, 538), interpreted as "the two (born) from the nose", referring to the nostrils of the divine mare of whom the two heavenly Knights are said to have been born, cf. Lommel *Vedische Skizzen*, 29-31: Saranyū, daughter of the smith god Tvastar, turned herself into a mare, and then sucked into her nostrils the seminal fluid which had been involuntarily spilled on the ground by the stallion into which the sun god Vivasvant had transformed himself. Hence the nasal birth.

[2] The Heavenly Twins were divinities of the so-called third function, relating to prosperity on earth, cf. Dumézil *op. cit.*, 36. In post-exile Jewish angelology the figure who is functionally closest to the Twins as a healer of men and women and champion of marriages is the archangel Raphael ("God heals"), described in *Tobit* 6 and 11. He is the adversary of the demon Asmodeus (*Tobit* 3:8; from the Iranian *Aēšma Daêva* "the Demon of fury"), enemy of marital union.

[3] Cf. Dumézil *op. cit.*, 79-80: "Suzanne et les vieillards".

[4] Cf. Dumézil *op. cit.*, 97-99. The first written mention of the Indo-European name of the Twins (*Nāsatyau*) appears in a treaty be-

and a Luristan bronze[1] of the 8th-7th century BC. But it is in the Indian *Mahābhārata* (iii, 123) that we have the first written record of the episode.[2]

> The mythical king Çaryāta gave his daughter Sukanyā[3] in marriage to a decrepit, very wise ascetic named Cyavana. One day the Heavenly Twins, coming down on earth, saw Sukanyā naked while she was bathing in the forest and, enchanted, asked her to consent to intercourse with one of them. When she refused, they plunged into the river, dragging old Cyavana after them, and when all three rose from the water young, handsome and identical in appearance, suggested to Sukanyā that she choose one of them as her partner. Sukanyā instinctively chose her husband, who repaid the Heavenly Twins for his recovered youth by telling them the secret of how to be accepted among the higher divinities. Satisfied, the Twins ascended into heaven.[4]

The Indian tale, and probably the archetype, turns on the motif of the attempted seduction of a chaste bride. Nevertheless, no ethical judgment is expressed with regard to the heavenly beings who are overcome with passion and sexual desire. Indeed, the episode turns out to be to their advantage, in the sense that, though disappointed of their earthly expectations, they achieve what is most dear to them in being admitted, in heaven, to the benefits of sacrificial oblation.

On the Iranian side, although no written text survives of this episode, we may imagine that popular tradition attributed an identical romance to the archangels Haurvatāt and Ameretāt. As we have seen, they are the direct descendants of the Dioscuri in that they too are benefactors of humanity. In the Iranian world,

---

tween the Hittite kingdom and the kingdom of Mitanni (14th century BC). The *Nashattiyana* are invoked along with the gods Mithra, Varuna and Indra as guarantors of an oath, cf. Thieme *Aryan Gods*, 314-315.

[1] Cf. Dumézil *op. cit.*, 87-96, photograph between 116-117; cf. Dussaud *Anciens bronzes*, 213, Fig. 11.

[2] Cf. Dumézil *op. cit.*, 34-49; *Mahābhārata*, 456-457.

[3] In Sanskrit the name Sukanyā means 'virtuous maiden' (*Su*-'good'), cf. Monier-Williams *Sanskrit Dictionary*, 1220, column 1.

[4] According to Dumézil, the two images mentioned above, on the gold vase of Hasanlu and on an embossed bronze plaque of Luristan, concern the miracle of the rejuvenation of Cyavana, an episode connected with the meeting of his wife Sukanyā with the Twins.

however, the situation changed radically, because in the meantime the religious reformation of Zoroaster (6th century BC) had taken place, and we know that this drastically altered the ancient Indo-Iranian pantheon. Some gods were changed into a sort of archangels; all the rest were lowered to the rank of devils. As new moral principles were affirmed, it is obvious that not even supernatural beings could be allowed a sexual weakness or an offence against the institution of matrimony. Thus Haurvatāt and Ameretāt were transformed into devils and severely punished.

It was probably in Mesopotamia, which had been under the influence of Persian culture since Achaemenid times, that the popular reworking of the myth of Sukanyā and the Dioscuri was passed on to the folklore of the Arabs and the Jews.[1]

In Arabia it was still in the nature of an apologue for the sacredness of marital union, whereas among the Jews, according to Dumézil, it followed two different paths. On the one hand, the episode merged into apocalyptic literature as part of the drama of the fall of the angels, one of the pillars of speculation about the origins of evil.[2] On the other, the legend was enriched with the themes of the 'lovely slandered woman' and the 'wise young man', and was adapted to new circumstances until it took on the connotations of the biblical tale of 'Susanna and the elders'.

It is my view that in Jewish apocalyptic literature there was a change of perspective with regard to the sin of the rebel angels. They were condemned not so much for failing in their specific task as 'Watchers', which also included the safeguarding of the marriage commitment between the men and women entrusted to them, as for triggering an ontological disorder by mingling two

---

[1] As to the Parthian epoch (2nd century BC - 3rd century AD), archaeology and philology have shown that there is no field in the spiritual and material life of Syria and Mesopotamia and the neighbouring countries that has not been influenced by Iranian culture, cf. Widengren *Iranisch-semitische Kulturbegegnung*.

[2] On the great themes debated by Jewish apocalyptics, especially in the so-called Enochian Pentateuch, see Paolo Sacchi's excellent introduction to the *Book of Enoch* in Sacchi *Apocrifi*, 423-461, and idem *Attesa*. With the *Book of the Watchers*, the oldest apocalyptic work (4th-3rd century BC), belief in life after death and in the preterhuman origin of evil (the sin of the angels and their fall) began. It is evil which implies the need for divine intervention for the redemption of humanity.

irreconcilable realities, the spiritual world of supernatural creatures and the corporal world of mortals.[1]

1.3 *The Falasha variant of the tale of Susanna*

The indigenous Jews of Ethiopia, the so-called Falasha, had a specific variant of the tale of Susanna, entitled *Gädlä Sosĕnna* – 'The Acts of Susanna' – though how and when this version developed is unknown. It was written in classical Ethiopic and is conserved in MS 8 (15th century) of the Faitlovitch Library in Tel Aviv.[2] It appears to be a late reworking of the corresponding text of the Septuagint, but contains two details which may go back to an older model.

> A king who had a daughter named Susanna (*Sosenna* or *Susĕnna*) gave her in marriage to another king. Widowed soon afterwards, Susanna received proposals of marriage from numerous sovereigns of kingdoms near and far. She turned them down because she wanted to devote herself exclusively to the service of the Lord her Creator. So three religious[3] came forward, each of them certain that he could marry her. When she rejected them because 'they are impure and transgress against the Law of the Lord', the three old men joined forces and falsely accused her of soliciting. Susanna's father was furious and orderd her to be thrown into a deep well. Susanna asked for the intervention of the Archangel Michael, making the sign of the Lord three times upon her face. Michael came at once in the form of a man and persuaded the king to interrogate each of the three old men separately. One said that he had seen Susanna fornicating under a fig tree; the second, in the royal palace; the third, in the women's apartments. When they were asked at what time of day Susanna had committed this sin, they could not answer. Susanna was cleared and seventy-seven kings elected her as queen over them.

Compared with the Greek Septuagint text and Theodotion's revision, the Falasha version presents substantial differences. The

---

[1] Cf. *Enoch* xv, 3-9, in Sacchi *Apocrifi*, 487-489.

[2] Cf. Wurmbrand *Falasha Susanna*, 32-34.

[3] The term used in classical Ethiopic is *rabbanāt*, the etymological equivalent of rabbis. In its Jewish sense this word means 'the elders (of the Jews)', cf. *Mark* 14:43; *Luke* 7:3; in its Christian sense it means 'the superiors (of monasteries)', cf. C.F.A. Dillmann, *Lexicon linguae aethiopicae*, Leipzig 1865 (reprint: New York 1955), column 287.

mise-en-scène is characteristic of folk tales: a king, a palace and a number of kingly suitors. The heroine's name is still Susanna, but she has been transformed into a young queen, recently widowed, and determined to give up the crown in order to devote herself to prayer. Moreover, Susanna's slanderers are more numerous: not two, but three, almost as if to increase the weight of their false testimony.[1]

One of the two details which may reflect an older model than the Septuagint story is represented by the figure who intervenes to save Susanna: the archangel Michael, who in the likeness of a man takes the place of Daniel.

This prompts two questions: 1) Why should the Falasha variant have excluded such a significant character as Daniel? 2) Is it correct, in any case, to conclude that Michael has taken Daniel's place? I should like to answer by putting a third question: Might it not be plausibly argued that Michael, the avenging angel *par excellence*, was already present in the archetype of the tale and had a significant role there?

This hypothesis is supported by the fact that the Septuagint version still assigns an important role to the 'angel of the Lord': it is he who gives Daniel the spirit of discernment and charges him to defend Susanna (v. 45); he is twice quoted in Daniel's speech to each of the false witnesses (vv. 55 and 59); and he finally reduces the two reprobates to ashes with a lightning bolt (v. 62).[2] It is only in Theodotion's reworking of the tale (2nd century AD) that the 'Angel of the Lord' is almost entirely eclipsed.[3] It is reasonable, then, to suppose that the archetype of the tale did not yet envisage the figure of Daniel and that the introduction of the young prophet led to a progressive marginalisation of the Archangel *ad maiorem Danielis gloriam*.[4] If the hypothesis that Susanna's wooers were originally angels (cf. Shemḥazay and 'Aza'el, § 1.2.1) is then

---

[1] According to *Deuteronomy* 17:6, the testimony of two or three witnesses was necessary for the imposition of the death sentence.

[2] Cf. Milik *Susanne à Qumrān*, 340.

[3] In Theodotion's recension the avenging angel is merely glanced at in young Daniel's threats to the old men: v. 55 "The angel of God has already received the sentence from God and will break you in two!", and v. 59 "Behold, the angel of God is waiting for you, sword in hand, to cut you in two and so make you die!".

[4] The expression is Wurmbrand's, *op. cit.*, 40.

accepted, it is easier to understand the reason for the intervention of the Archangel Michael, traditionally considered the proudest adversary of the rebel angels, always watchful and attentive to the re-establishment of order and justice.

The second detail in the Falasha variant which is worthy of attention is the fact that the judge in charge of the hearing asks each of the witnesses two questions, and that they answer both. This is a particularly interesting circumstance because on this point the Greek Septuagint text seems corrupt or at least inconsistent. The witnesses are asked two questions (though the second of these is not the same as in the Falasha variant), but they answer only the first. As to Theodotion's version, the inconsistency is resolved by having only one question and one answer.[1] In this case too it may be deduced that the Falasha variant more faithfully reflects the structure of the archetype of the tale, which presumably had two questions and two answers.[2] For the second time we are in the presence of a process of evolution which starts with the Falasha variant and ends with Theodotion's revision.

There is another reason why the Falasha variant of the tale of Susanna is important: it inaugurates the narrative motif of the young woman who consecrates herself to the service of God, a motif which, as we shall see (§§ 3 and 4.3.3), was to be the forerunner of further interesting developments.

2 The story of Susanna in Arab-Islamic culture

2.1 *The Susanna of the Tazyīn al-aswāq*

The only text in Arab literature, as far as is known, which relates the well-known biblical story under the name of Susanna forms part of the work entitled *Tazyīn al-aswāq fī akhbār al-'uššāq*[3] by the Syrian writer Dāwud al-Antākī (16th century), who makes specific reference to the *Book of Daniel*, but alters it to some extent and adds something of his own. For a start, Susanna

[1] Cf. note 2, p. 10.

[2] On this matter, see also § 2.2.

[3] Beirut edition, undated, Dār wa-Maktabat al-Hilāl, 280-281. The title means 'The embellishment of the markets with stories of lovers'. The biblical tale is cited by Dāwud as an example of reprehensible behaviour by a lover.

(in the Arab text *Sūsan* or *Sawsan*) is promoted to the rank of queen, since her husband Joakim is identified with Jehoiachin, penultimate king of Judah, deported by Nebuchadnezzar to Babylon in 597 BC (II Kings 24:15; 25:27). Secondly, the two judges present themselves with their official rods in order to make the young queen uneasy; thirdly, we are told that Daniel was thirteen years old at the time. Finally, the tree under which Susanna is supposed to have committed adultery is claimed to have been either a terebinth or an olive. As in the Greek Septuagint text,[1] but unlike Theodotion's revision, the false witnesses are consumed by a fire from heaven.

In making Susanna the wife of King Jehoiachin, Dāwud al-Antākī must have accepted a Jewish tradition drawn on 300 years earlier by Jerahmeel ben Solomon, in chapter 65 of whose *Chronicles* (12th century)[2] Susanna's husband is called Jehoiachin like the exiled king. It is true that there is not the least hint at her royal dignity, but Susanna is described as daughter of Shealtiel, of the House of David, known as the father of Zerubbabel, the future king-governor of Jerusalem (Haggai 1:1; Esra 3:2), making Susanna Zerubbabel's sister. There is also an allusion to King Jehoiachin and Susanna as husband and wife in the *Midrash Rabbah* of Leviticus.[3]

2.2 *The 'Susanna' of the Thousand and One Nights*

A condensed version of the biblical tale – barely a page – is to be found, as I have said, in some editions, of Egyptian origin, of

---

[1] See vv. 60-62a "Then the angel of the Lord threw fire among them".

[2] Cf. Gaster *Jerahmeel*, 202-205.

[3] Cf. Freedman-Simon *Midrash Rabbah*, IV, § xix, 6, 248-249; Wurmbrand *Falasha Susanna*, 35. Semiramis asks her husband Nebuchadnezzar to allow Jehoiachin, long shut up in a tower, to be reunited with his wife, who on meeting him demurely says: *kᵉ-šōšannāh adummāh rā'ītī* ("I have seen something like a red lily"), which tells him that she is haemorrhaging. Hearing this, the devout king of Judah abstains from intercourse with her. The name Susanna (Hebrew *Šōšannāh*) means 'lily'; according to Milik *Susanne à Qumrān*, 354, it is rather the name of the city of Susa (*Šūšān*), capital of Elam, for in olden times the names of cities were often given to little girls.

the *Thousand and One Nights*.[1] The heroine's name is no longer remembered.

> Two old keepers of the temple garden laid a trap for a virtuous Israelite woman, who was in the habit of going into the garden to perform her ritual ablutions there. When she rejected their advances, they accused the woman of having committed adultery with a young man who, they said, had managed to escape. The woman was condemned to death by stoning, but while they were taking her to be executed, the prophet Daniel, then only twelve years old, rose in her defence. Obtaining permission to re-examine the case, the boy questioned the two witnesses separately. One identified the scene of the misdemeanour as the eastern corner of the garden, where a pear-tree grew, while the other identified the western corner, where an apple-tree grew. The slanderers were killed by a lightning bolt.

At this point the biblical story, extensively reworked, has been transformed into a popular tale. There are three innovations:

a) the setting is Jerusalem instead of Babylon, and Susanna is thus reduced to an anonymous female figure; b) in consequence, the social status of the two slanderers is likewise reduced: instead of being 'Elders of the people', they become old keepers of the Temple garden; c) Daniel's age is specified as twelve, where the Bible merely describes him as a youngster.[2]

Though so brief, the anecdote contains one very interesting detail, which is only found in the Greek Septuagint text. The boy puts a two-part question to each of the keepers: a) under what tree, and b) in what part of the garden they caught Susanna making love with the unidentified young man. This same pair of questions is put by Daniel in the Septuagint version (vv. 55 and 59), though in the Greek text each of the two false witnesses answers only the question about the tree. This, in my view, amounts to proof that the Arabian text of the *Thousand and One Nights* is dependent not on the Greek text of the tale of Susanna, but rather on the pre-

---

[1] Cf. Burton *Thousand Nights*, IV, n.° 60.

[2] Cf. the Septuagint text, *Daniel* 13:45: παιδάριον νεώτερον. However, Daniel is presented as a twelve-year-old boy also in a Syriac version of the tale of Susanna, cf. Wurmbrand *Falasha Susanna*, 40, note 2.

sumed original text in Hebrew or Aramaic, which must have been lost.[1]

The mention of the lightning bolt which strikes the false witnesses is interesting too, since this is a detail found only in the Greek Septuagint text and may have belonged to the Semitic original. In 1899 Chauvin[2] put forward the hypothesis that this anecdote, together with others, also on Jewish topics, which have been absorbed in the *Thousand and One Nights*, goes back to the book *al-Isrā'īlīyāt* ('Israelite matters'), by the famous Yemenite traditionalist Wahb bin Munabbih (b. 654-5, d. 728~732 AD). R. Georges Khoury, who has made an in-depth study of Wahb bin Munabbih's works, has not, however, found any trace of our story.[3]

It is unfortunately impossible to establish the period in which the anecdote was inserted in the *Thousand and One Nights*. Papyrological research has, however, shown that this work was fixed in written form as early as the second half of the 8th century, in other words in the first decades of the reign of the Abbasids.[4]

2.3 *The 'Susanna' of the Story of David*

In one of Islam's oldest narrative works there is an episode which beyond a shadow of a doubt represents the most profane and the crudest of the collateral versions of the biblical tale of Susanna. This is the *Ḥadīth Dāwud* or *Story of David*, attributed to Wahb bin Munabbih. We owe the discovery of this extremely important source to R. Georges Khoury, who published it in 1972.[5]

---

[1] On the problem of the original text in Aramaic, see Milik *Susanne à Qumrān*. The structural detail of the twofold question followed by a twofold answer is also included in the Falasha variation of the tale of Susanna, cf. § 1.3.

[2] Chauvin *Récension égyptienne*, 57-58, and *Bibliographie*, IV, 216, and VI, note 1, 193.

[3] Cf. Khoury *Légendes prophétiques*, idem *Wahb b. Munabbih*.

[4] Cf. Khoury *Mille et Une Nuits*, 33.

[5] Khoury *Wahb b. Munabbih*, 1, 96-101 (GD 23, line 19 - GD 25, line 16). The *Story of David* has been preserved in two papyri: as an independent work in a text dated 229 of the Hegira (843/844 AD), and as part of the *Kitāb bad' al-khalq wa-qiṣaṣ al-anbiyā'* "Book of the beginning of creation and of the prophetic legends", written by the Persian man of letters Wathīma bin Mūsā bin al-Furāt al-Fārisī and passed down by his

> The first time King David became aware of the wisdom of his son Solomon was on the following occasion. A very attractive single woman appealed to a judge to solve a dispute; the judge said he was prepared to deal with the matter on condition that she would agree to marry him. When she turned him down, the judge tried to rape her. Disillusioned, the young woman went in turn to the head of the guards, the inspector of the markets and the king's grand chamberlain. All three behaved as the judge had done. Losing faith in the justice of men, the woman gave up the attempt to defend her rights. One day the four dignitaries met at court and the conversation turned to their meeting with this woman: fearing that she might expose them, they decided to rid themselves of her with a slanderous accusation: that she had had carnal relations with her dog. David, horrified, did not hesitate to pronounce the death sentence. Hearing of this matter, young Solomon set out on horseback with his companions and staged a hearing in court, assigning the various parts to his friends and himself taking the role of the judge. Separating the four witnesses, he asked each of them what colour the dog was. The first said it was black, the second reddish, the third white and the fourth grey. Going back to the palace with his companions, Solomon told his father of the results of his questioning. The king learned the lesson and summoned the four dignitaries who had accused the woman. In the course of questioning them, he received independently the same conflicting answers as his son had anticipated; so the four slanderers were stoned in place of the innocent woman.

In the first years of Islam, then, a story must have been circulating which had been distantly inspired by the affair of Susanna, in which there is the motif of boys who act out a trial for fun.[1] Among them, one is destined to become a pre-Islamic prophet, and this, in fact, is how the Muslims regard Solomon.[2]

---

son 'Umāra bin Wathīma bin Mūsā (d. 289/902), cf. Khoury *Légendes prophétiques*, 123-126; idem *Codification*, 113-114. Both these papyri are in the Schott-Reinhardt collection in Heidelberg.

[1] The motif of the king who finds the solution to a difficult juridical case by watching youngsters at play and who then asks the brightest of them to preside over the real court is widespread in Jewish folklore, cf. Schwarzbaum *Biblical legends*, 155, note 157, and Gaster *Daughter of Amram*, 209. In the *Thousand and One Nights* this motif appears in the story of Ali Khoja, a Baghdad merchant, cf. Galland *Mille e una notte*, IV, 249-265.

[2] Cf. *Koran* iv, 163.

We shall return to this motif in due course (§ 4.3.1). Note that here, for the first time, the vectors of the affair are reversed. The old men – now four in number – no longer approach the heroine, for it is she who needs their help in a legal matter, rather as in the Islamic legend of Hārūt and Mārūt (§ 1.2.2). It is probable that the lovely woman accused of bestiality was engaged in commerce, since she also appealed to the inspector of markets. This means that she was not of noble lineage, but she was moved by the same determination as the Falasha princess not to marry. We do not know, in fact, whether she was a widow like the princess, or as yet unmarried.

2.4 *The Story of the skull and the king*

The Arabic manuscript translated here emerged in the course of research on the oriental manuscripts preserved in the *Forschungs- und Landesbibliothek* in Gotha. The purpose of this research was to collect the Arabic manuscripts of this Thuringian city regarding the legend known as *Jesus and the skull.*[1] Among the many witnesses to this legend, Pertsch, author of the catalogue of oriental codices in Gotha, had also mistakenly included MS orient. A 2756, folios 30a-44b, an unpublished text, undated and of unknown authorship.[2]

---

[1] Cf. Levi Della Vida *Gesù e il teschio*, 196-201; Chauvin *Récension égyptienne*, No. 23, 75-76; Khoury *Wahb b. Munabbih*, I, 244, 253. The research in question was carried out by Bianca Torta for her degree dissertation "La leggenda islamica del teschio redivivo nelle fonti arabe", presented at the University of Turin on October 11, 1994.

[2] Pertsch *Gotha*, IV, 464. The text is found in an undated miscellaneous manuscript, consisting of 176 pages (20.5 x 15 cm; 13 lines per page). The codex is written in a clear, fairly recent *naskhī* style, almost entirely vocalised. It contains thirteen texts (*pace* Pertsch, who counts twelve), including the one which interests us here; they deal with traditions, stories of mystics, and prayers. The text which precedes the *Story of the skull and the king* is the story of the prophet Ṣāliḥ and his she-camel (*Ḥadīth Ṣāliḥ wa-n-nāqa*, fol. 1b-30a); the text which follows it is an episode from the life of the great Persian mystic Abū Yazīd al-Bistāmī, d. 874 (fol. 44b-52a). The last text describes the meeting between the *ṣūfī* ʻAbdullāh bin al-Mubāraka (d. 796) and the famous lady mystic Rābiʻa al-ʻAdawīya (d. 801): *Ḥadīth ʻAbdillāh bin al-Mubāraka maʻa Rābiʻa al-ʻAdawīya*.

What probably misled him was the title of the text in question, *Ḥadīth al-jumjuma maʿa l-malik*, 'Story of the skull and the king', which is very similar to one of the titles of the legend of *Jesus and the skull*: *Ḥadīth al-jumjuma maʿa ʿÎsā.*[1] This Arabic expression can, in fact, mean the conversation between a human skull and a king. While, however, the legend of *Jesus and the skull* is entirely built around the questions Christ puts to the talking skull of an ancient sovereign, in the *Story of the skull and the king* a skull does appear, but does not say a word.

In reality the *Story of the skull and the king* has very little in common with that of *Jesus and the skull.* It is a remarkable tale which has all the formal requirements to appear in the *Thousand and One Nights* (a folksy style, fabulous descriptions, *coups de théâtre*, insertion of verses commenting on the story) and which in addition unexpectedly includes a reworking of the story of Susanna.

3 The *Story of the skull and the king* translated from the Arabic[2]

(folio 30a) In the name of God, Merciful and Compassionate, it is said that in the time of a king of the Israelites there was a mighty king who had a flock of courtiers and who was famed for his faith and his piety towards the King Judge. For a long time he led the pleasantest and most delightful life. He was a famous hunter and went out on hunting expeditions that lasted one month and ten days.

One day, deciding to go hunting, the king left his palace and commanded his servants to make ready their mounts, prepare the food, bring the cheetahs, the falcons and the trained eagles and hawks (fol. 30b) and all the hunting weapons. Accompanied by soldiers and servants with greyhounds, the king travelled for a day and a night, until in the morning he came to a splendid area that shone like silver, with few inhabitants and rich in plants and leafy trees. There saffron grew, and red anemones, and on the heights

---

[1] Cf. Levi Della Vida *Vaticano*, 185: MS. No. 1191/3.

[2] MS Gotha (*Forschungs- und Landesbibliotek*) A 2756, foll. 30a-44b.

bamboo canes were shooting up.[1] The place was striking for the number and dimensions of its streams, which were not easy to ford. In the centre grew a tree with a tall leafy top where all kinds of birds lived: turtledoves, thrushes, nightingales, stockdoves and starlings.

The king was enchanted by such beauty, and commanded his followers to strike camp there. When the poles had been fixed and the pavilions raised, (fol. 31a) some of the company scattered among the trees, some went hunting for birds, some fishing in the streams, while those in charge of the cheetahs leapt into the saddle because the place was rich in iguanas, hares and wild cattle. Game was abundant, and there were many fish in the streams. Lighting fires, they dined on gazelles, fish and gamebirds.

The king remained there about ten days, until one day he mounted his horse 'Uqāb,[2] whose mane was red as the rising sun and whose hooves were of iron or stone. It galloped like a stormy sea and like the wind that stirs up the dust; it had the disposition of a wolf and the speed (fol. 31b) of the gazelle. The birds did not follow it, preferring to avoid it. The king was wearing a brightly polished Indian breastplate; in his hands were a long spear and a shield of padded leather,[3] and he wore a magnificent cloak.[4]

As he was wandering among the trees and the gardens, he saw a graceful white gazelle, bearing on its back brocade drapery; round its neck were an amber necklace and a jewelled collar, and in its ears were two jewels that shone like the sun. As soon as he saw it, the king found it stupendous, and thinking that it had run away from a royal palace, wanted to take possession of it himself. So he spurred his horse, which dashed forward like an eagle or a stormcloud, doing all it could to follow the gazelle. Meanwhile the soldiers had lost sight of him because he had gone off without

---

[1] Saffron and red anemones appear frequently in the *Thousand and One Nights* as elements in the description of fabulous landscapes. Cf. for saffron Mahdi *Alf Layla wa-Layla*, 1, 62nd night, 198, line 9; for red anemones, 28th night, 127, line 19.

[2] In Arabic the name 'Uqāb means 'eagle'.

[3] The Arabic adjective which I translate 'padded' is written *tanbatīya*, a senseless word which may be the result of a miswriting of *tanbaqīya*. In R. Dozy *Supplément*, I, Leyde 1881, 152b, this word is recorded with the meaning 'bonnet sans poil, rembourré de coton'.

[4] This is an *ad sensum* translation of an adjective which is difficult to read.

them. (fol. 32a) As the gazelle stopped every time the king wanted to stop, his longing to capture it increased, and he immediately galloped after it again. At last they came to the foot of a huge mountain under which was the opening to a cave. The gazelle ran in and the king, dismounting, followed. But he found not the least trace of it in the cave, and was very displeased, for both he and his horse had tired themselves in vain.

As he was wandering crossly about the cave, he caught sight of a huge weatherworn skull, than which he had never seen anything more terrifying. Walking round and round it, he was amazed at its size, and said: 'I wish I knew what was the worst torment inflicted on this skull! Was it the attack of the worms or the oppression of the tomb, the earth poured on top of it or the torments of Gehenna and the fierce heat (fol. 32b) of the fires? I wish I knew who this skull belonged to! A king or a nobleman, an abject or a respectable man, a poor man or a rich one?' The king continued to marvel at its size and at the span of its arched brows. His intellect grew proud, putting his heart in jeopardy, because disbelief in the Most High had become manifest in him. In fact he said: 'I think this skull will never come back to life. It will no longer be able to eat or drink, nor live in comfort, nor cause suffering any longer.' Then he lifted it up, put it on his horse and rejoined his entourage.

The king spent the whole night in that place meditating, and when dawn broke he mounted his horse, returned to the city and went back into his palace.There he assembled the wise men, the philosophers and the scholars, put the skull on a golden receptacle and showed it to them, saying: 'What do you say, (fol. 33a) o gathering of wise men, about this skull? Do you think it will eat and drink again, make merry and sing, cause suffering or show goodness of heart? That is not possible, it is truly inconceivable!' The wise men expressed their judgment, because in them too doubt had been insinuated regarding the power of God. So the king called his gardener and told him to take the skull and keep it with him in the garden until he was asked for it. The gardener took it, dug a pit in the garden and buried it there.

Then God – He is Mighty and Sublime – made both him and the king forget it.[1] God – blessed and exalted be He – meant in fact to perform a marvel. From that skull He made a shoot spring

[1] The text is corrupt and there is an erasure after the eulogy.

up, which grew and grew until it became a great tree which produced fruits that looked (fol. 33b) like quinces and tasted like pears.[1] One day the gardener approached this tree and was astonished at its form and its beauty. The man, who was greatly advanced in years, reached out to the tree and plucked a fruit, ate it and found it full of flavour. After a short time, the hairs of his head and his beard fell out and he became beardless again and recovered his former energy. Again he reached out for another fruit and became a handsome young man with a heavy black beard.

So he put three fruits on a tray, covered them with a silk napkin and went to the king in his palace. Here the guards asked him: 'What do you do?' He replied: 'I am So-and-So, the gardener.' So they presented him to the king, (fol. 34a) who said to him: 'Tell me what you have to say and explain what has happened to you! For you were old, but today you have become young!' He answered: 'O my lord, in the garden a tall tree has sprung up, with a broad trunk and many branches, and this is its fruit.' The king looked at it and was filled with wonder. After this the gardener said to him: 'O my lord, I plucked one of these fruits, ate it and thus the years fell away from me!' So he explained all that had happened.

The king, in his turn, took one of these fruits, ate it and felt his body become stronger, his heart rejoice and his vigour increase. So he ordered a portico[2] to be built beside the tree and lamps to be hung from its branches. They perfumed it (fol. 34b) with various essences, lit camphor candles under it[3] and made

---

[1] The flavour of the pear, like that of the quince, is highly regarded in the *Thousand and One Nights*, cf. Mahdi *Alf Layla wa-Layla*, 1, 61st night, 196, line 17.

[2] An arcade or a pavilion with columns. The term used in Arabic is *miḥrāb*, which normally designates the niche in a mosque indicating the direction a Muslim must face when praying. As certain passages in the Koran *miḥrāb* (iii, 37, 39; xix, 11) refer to places of prayer in Jerusalem visited by Mary the mother of Jesus or by Zechariah, other passages (xxxiv, 13; xxxviii, 21) to the palaces of David and Solomon, it may originally have meant the colonnade of the inner courtyard of a sacred building, or of the central atrium of a residence, cf. Serjeant *Miḥrāb*, and G. Fehérvári, under "Miḥrāb" in *E.I.*², VII, 1993, 7-15. In addition, *miḥrāb* may indicate the altar of a Christian church, perhaps together with its ciborium.

[3] The motif of the portico, the hanging lamps and the scented or

votive offerings to it. Finally the king appointed a guardian to protect it.

If an old man ate its fruits, he regained his youth; if a sick man ate them, he rose at once and was healed; if he were blind, he regained his sight. From all around came impressive offerings and no one failed to bring perfumes and candles.

The king's daughter, whose name was ar-Rabāb,[1] hearing of this matter, said to her father: 'Father, I dearly want to see this tree, pray by it and take it a votive offering.' So the king ordered his servants to put up huge tents in the garden around the tree. These were duly mounted and carpets laid inside them. The next morning (fol. 35a) the girl went out with her mother, her nurses and her handmaidens, as well as those who were dear to her, her train and her servants, and all rejoiced on seeing the garden. Ar-Rabāb ate a little fruit, then drew near to the tree to examine its fruits, plucked one and ate it.

Having remained in the garden until sunset, she went back to the palace, but two days later her face grew pale, her belly grew large and she changed colour. At once the news spread and so her mother visited her, but the girl denied her condition. Then her mother said to her: 'My daughter, tell me your story and what has happened to you. My daughter, is it possible that a man has approached you?'. She answered, 'Before God, mother, no one has approached me, nor has anything happened to me unless at the moment when I ate that fruit in the garden (fol. 35b) and what you see happened.'

Her mother, puzzled, went to the king, greeted him and he returned her greeting and invited her to be seated. Sitting down, she told him of the problem of her daughter ar-Rabāb and what had happened to her. The king was greatly disturbed on hearing these words and commanded them to bring the girl to him. The handmaidens called her and she presented herself, greeting him. He said: 'My daughter, be truthful in your words! Has not someone of your acquaintance approached you to hurt you?' But she answered him as she had answered her mother. So the king said to her mother: 'Call the nurses to examine her!' She went out

---

camphor candles is repeatedly found in the *Thousand and One Nights*, in exotic settings, cf. Mahdi *Alf Layla wa-Layla*, 1, 62th night, 198, lines 9-12; 64th night, 204, lines 11, 21-22.

[1] In Arabic the name ar-Rabāb means 'white cloud'.

and sent someone to call them. They arrived (fol. 36a) and confirmed that the girl was still a virgin with the seal of her Lord, Him who is mighty and exalted.

When they told the king this, he sank into a sea of thoughts, went into the garden, approached the tree, looked closely at it and saw that it had changed and grown yellow. So he called the keeper of the garden and asked him about the skull. The man was perplexed and bewildered for the space of an hour, then he dug beside the tree and there was the skull, with the roots of the tree adhering to the centre of its crown.[1] Then the king understood that the Most High had shown him his might through his daughter. Going back into the palace, he assembled the scholars, the wise men and the philosophers in whose hearts a doubt had insinuated itself regarding God – He is mighty and exalted – (fol. 36b) and showed them the skull. They were astonished, and understood that God is omnipotent.

Meanwhile ar-Rabāb reached the ninth month of her pregnancy and had strong labour pains: her right side opened below the ribs and out came a female child as beautiful as the day. But the king's daughter died at the same hour and at the same instant. The king was deeply troubled and commanded her to be dressed in her loveliest robe and buried, and he wept bitterly.

One day when the king, seated on his throne, was surrounded by the greatest powers of the kingdom who were comforting him, all at once the gardener came in, saying: 'O king, God has wanted to console you by intervening on the tree: it has withered up!' This surprised the king and all those present. He understood that God – may the mention of Him be exalted and His names sanctified – is a just judge whom nothing escapes.

The king ordered the nurses, the handmaidens (fol. 37a) and the wet nurses to bring the baby up, and called her Susanna.[2] In time she grew, and when she was twelve years old she went to the king and greeted him. The king asked her to sit down, and when she was seated [she asked him] who her father was. So the king

---

[1] Literally "and the skull appeared and the tree in the middle of the crown of the skull". The Arabic word for crown of the skull (*yāfūkh*) may also indicate the bregmatic fontanelle or the meeting point of the coronal suture and the sagittal.

[2] Susanna (in the Arabic text *Sawsana*) is derived from the Arabic *sawsan* or *sūsan* 'lily'; this word appears in the *Thousand and One Nights* as *sawsān*, cf. Mahdi *Alf Layla wa-Layla*, I, 28th night, 127, line 19.

told her the story of the skull and the tree, of how his heart had been invaded by doubt regarding the Most High, how his daughter had eaten the fruit, had become pregnant by it and how she herself had issued from below her ribs.

The story greatly astonished the girl, who said: 'O king, I must absolutely serve, praise, glorify, exalt and proclaim to be holy Him who created me without the intervention of a father. For that reason, I earnestly beg you to build me a cloister with trees and a raised cell, where I can serve God (fol. 37b) until the moment when I go to him.' The king immediately commanded what she had described to be built and called workers from all around. Thus the cell was built for her as she asked and desired.

So she put on a woollen tunic[1] and went to live in that cell and that cloister, where the king had had everything taken that she might need. He also assigned three handmaidens to her, to serve her while she was reciting the Psalms. The girl's voice was so extraordinarily lovely that the birds, enchanted by its tunefulness, came to perch on her head. All the servants of God came to visit her from every region, and were astonished at the sweetness of her voice.

Not far away was a huge monastery with a multitude of servants of God and ascetics. Alongside it was a cell in which lived (fol. 38a) two servants of God, one of whom was called Hiram[2] and the other Huraym.[3] They served God – He is mighty and exalted – with great purity of life, and reciting the Psalms in sweet voices. One day they both came down from their cell and went to where the girl was. They greeted her, and she, returning their greeting, asked them: 'O holy ascetics, what has made you come down from your cell?' They answered: 'We came down to visit you and hear your recitation [of the Psalms].' So she recited some Psalms for them and they, marvelling, went back to their cell. But in their hearts a great passion for the girl burst out and

---

[1] Reference to the rough woollen tunic (*ṣūf* 'wool') which Islamic ascetics wore; for this reason they were called *ṣūfī* 'the wool people' (cf. sufic, sufism).

[2] The name Hiram is connected in Arabic with the nominalised adjective *harim*, meaning 'decrepit old man', referring to the advanced age of the two old men who tried to seduce and slandered Susanna. In the Greek of the Septuagint they are called οἱ πρεσβύτεροι 'the elders'.

[3] The name Huraym is the diminutive of the Arabic *harim*, see note 1: 'little old man'.

they became infatuated with her to the point that neither their lips nor their tongues mentioned the name of the Most High any longer, so that the accursed devil stepped in between them. In fact the next morning Hiram and Huraym met with the devil.

(fol. 38b) Hiram said to Huraym: 'I did not hear you recite or speak yesterday.' Huraym retorted: 'Neither did I hear you recite or pray. What happened to you?' He answered: 'Before God, o my brother, that girl has stolen my heart, and my passion for her has mingled with my limbs.' Huraym replied: 'The same thing has happened to me, my brother. What trap shall we lay for her?' He replied: 'Let us go to her, you and I, and invite her to come down, and when she comes down we shall have our way with her.'

So they went down from their cell, went to Susanna's cell and greeted her. She returned their greeting and welcomed them. Then they said to her: 'O Susanna, will you not come down to us so that we may rejoice in the happy opportunity of seeing you?' She came down to them and brought them food. (fol. 39a) They ate and talked together for an hour.

But when she was about to rise, they leapt on her and seized her. So she said: 'Why are you seizing me, what do you mean to do?' The two replied: 'You are in our power.' 'That suits me very well', she answered, 'have you not realised that I persuaded the king to build me this cell and this cloister and that I came to live here because my heart was infatuated with you? With that pretext, my plan was fulfilled when the king built me this cell, where I can live alone now and do as I please. But I do not think that this is the place you want. Whichever of you wishes to come first, please do come up with me to my cell!' The two believed her words and so she added: 'I shall go up first (fol. 39b) to make the place ready and shall stay there alone for a moment.' They answered: 'Do just as you choose.'

So Susanna rose, went up to her cell, barred the door and barricaded herself inside with rocks. Then she climbed up above the cell and said: 'O enemies of God, you have served Him in vain! Before God, you deserve the fire! After serving and praying God for seven hundred years you have rebelled against Him. Stay away from me! May God curse you!'

The two men went away, furious with her because she had managed to get away from them, and they consulted each other as to what they should do. Hiram said: 'O brother, let us go into the city and tell the king the girl's story. So that he may condemn her to the pyre, we shall say that she was fornicating and that we hastened to denounce her.' They both set off (fol. 40a) till they reached the city and when people recognised them, they approached, greeted them and asked for their blessing. Then they asked them what they wanted and what had driven them to leave their cell. They answered: 'A matter to be expounded to the king.'

After this they went to the king's palace, entered and greeted him. He did them honour, greeted them and asked what had driven them to leave their cell. They answered: 'O king, it is you who have driven us to come down, because it is you who made a sinful woman live near us! We are certain of this, for we are eyewitnesses. As soon as it was possible, we came to tell you what we saw, because we have proof that she is on the road to perdition.' The king said: 'Your story is believable and deserves to be trusted. How do you want her to die?' They said: 'Send her to burn at the stake!' The king said that, if it was the will of the Most High, he would do it the very next day. So the two servants of God went away, but the king spent a night in deep anguish because of the girl, wondering how he should behave.

As soon as morning came he mounted his horse 'Uqāb, and, ordering his men to amass faggots in a large square, he set off heavy-hearted to seek a little relief in the woods and orchards. And so he passed by a green garden, glanced towards it and glimpsed a stretch of running water. Dismounting, he slaked his thirst and cooled his hands and face in the water, (fol. 41a) but he soon realised that six youths were approaching, carrying faggots on their heads, and that they must be thirsty. The king said to himself: 'These young men must be tired, but if they saw me they would go without water, so that I would be guilty of a sin and a fault.' So he rose and hid behind the wall of a ruin. Then he prepared to listen to what the young men would say.

Once they had arrived, the young men threw their bundles on the ground, stripped and swam in the stretch of water, then came out, dressed, took out the bread they had with them and ate. When they had finished eating, one of them said: 'Let us rise, brothers! Let us hurry to see the burning of Susanna at the stake and how the king reacts to the fact that the two servants of God Hiram and Huraym (fol. 41b) have seen her fornicating and have come to report what they have seen. Another youth said: 'Before God, o brothers, my heart cannot bear to see dying in the fire a holy pure woman who is a servant of God and an ascetic.' The other youths replied: 'Yet those two servants of God testify that she was fornicating.' 'Before God, brothers', he said, 'those two are lying and are guilty! Do you want to ascertain the truth of my words?' 'Yes!' they replied. 'Then one of you play the part of Hiram and another play the part of Huraym!' They agreed.

So the young man called the first of the two to appear before him, while the other remained at a distance, and asked him: 'Did you see Susanna while she was fornicating?' 'Yes!' he answered. 'And who was fornicating with her?' He replied: 'It was a young man with a black beard, dark-complexioned, tall and good-looking.' 'Go back to your place!' he ordered, and made (fol. 42a) the second come, to whom he said: 'O Huraym, did you see Susanna while she was fornicating?' 'Yes!' he answered. 'Describe the man who was fornicating with her.' He answered: 'He was a smooth-skinned youth, beardless, with no down on his cheeks, light-complexioned, short and good-looking.' So the young man said: 'You see, brothers, how your evidence conflicts. You were lying. The testimonies of Hiram and Huraym will conflict in the same way.'

When the king heard their words he rejoiced greatly, came out from his hiding place, greeted them and said to the young man: 'My son, come with me to judge the two servants of God as you have just done!' The young man answered: 'O king, do you not see my status and the condition in which I find myself? I am not fit to judge people.' So the king said: 'I will have a robe made to fit you and I will have you wear the cap and gown so that you can sit in judgment.' He answered: 'I shall do (fol. 42b) so, if God wills.' The king then went back to the city and commanded the people to assemble the next morning. When dawn broke and the sun rose he sent for the young man, made him put on the robe of an advocate, put the cap and gown on him, had a fine seat brought for him and invited him to sit on it.

When the leading figures of the country, the ascetics and the servants of God had gathered together, the young man ordered the servants of God Hiram and Huraym to be brought in. They came and sat down near him. Then the young man said to them: 'O Hiram and Huraym, did you see Susanna while she was fornicating?' 'Yes', they replied, 'we saw her several times with our own eyes.' The young man turned to those present and said to them: 'Have you taken note of what they said?' They said that they had. So the young man ordered the two to be separated. The order was carried out, and each was put in a separate place without his companion.

Then he had Hiram appear alone (fol. 43a) and said to him: 'O Hiram, did you see Susanna while she was fornicating?' 'Yes!' he replied. 'Who was it who was fornicating with her? What did he look like?' He answered: 'He was a smooth-skinned, beardless young man without down on his cheeks, fair-skinned, short and good-looking.' He asked further: 'What time was it when you saw her?' He said: 'I saw her at midday and she did not go away until sunset.' So the young man ordered him to be taken back to his place, and this was done.

Then he summoned Huraym, who stood erect in front of him. The young man said to him: 'Tell me nothing but the truth!' The other assured him that he would. So he asked him: 'Are you testifying that the servant of God Susanna prostituted herself and fornicated?' 'Yes!' he answered. He asked him: 'Did you see her with your own eyes?' 'Yes!' he answered. He asked further: 'And who was she fornicating with?' He answered: 'With a black-bearded man, dark-skinned (fol. 43b) and tall of stature.' Then he asked: 'At what time did you see her?' He answered: 'At sunset and at dawn, when she went away'.

So the young man exclaimed: 'Before God, you have both lied! I declare you guilty!' The crowd asked the king to put them to death, but the young man said: 'Do not inflict a quick death on them, because you would give them relief! Send them rather to the pyre, as they wanted you to do to that holy pure girl, servant of God and ascetic!' So they made them both come and forced them to confess their guilt and to admit that Satan himself had driven them to commit the crime they had committed.

When the crowd heard this, they stoned them, and tying them up with ropes they took them and threw them into the pit that had been dug for Susanna. They stacked faggots in it (fol. 44a) and set fire to them. The fire blazed for so long that they were reduced to ashes.

The king then turned to the young man and asked him: 'My son, who is your father?' He answered: 'It is Zechariah,[1] peace be

---

[1] This is Zechariah, father of John the Baptist (cf. *Luke* 1:5-25), whom Islam regards as a prophet of equal importance to his sons (*Yaḥyā*), cf. *Koran* iii, 37-41; vi, 85; xix, 2-11; xxi, 89-90. Hence, according to this tale, the youth who saved Susanna was not Daniel, but John the Baptist.

upon him!' The king said to him: 'You are right; such a fruit can only come from such a plant!' Then he gave him splendid robes and gave him a lovely girl as his bride. As a moral, the epigram was recited which tells of the man who one day dug a pit of which he had reason to repent:

> If you want to dig a pit, make sure that it is wide!
> Be indulgent with young people, if they are inexperienced,
> But don't accept excuses from those who have grey hair.

Immediately afterwards, accompanied by ministers, officials and army officers, the king set out on horseback, reached the cloister where Susanna lived and, going up to her, told her the story of the two servants of God Hiram and Huraym who (fol. 44b) lived near her. The girl's comment was:

> In vain does man exert himself if with God he is not contented.

Then the king said goodbye to her and went back to the city, while the girl continued to serve the Most High till her last hour came. When she died, the king grieved for her for a long time, wrapped her in a linen cloth and buried her beside her mother. Then he withdrew his heart from the world, took the crown from his head and the diadem from his brow and, abdicating in favour of his son, went up to the cloister where Susanna had lived. There he served God – He is mighty and exalted – with great fervour until his last hour came, and when he died God had mercy on him.

End of the story

4 *Antecedents and parallelisms*

The story of the skull and the king is a didactic novella with the colourfulness and style of a fantastic folk tale. It is in three parts of varying length.

From the first of these parts (fol. 30a-32a) the marvellous is already in evidence with the description of a dreamlike landscape where a hunt is in progress. The protagonist, as a well-established Near East narrative and figurative convention demands, is a 'hunter king';[1] we are not told his name, but we do know the name

[1] The first hunter king is the biblical Nimrod, king of Babel, Erech

of his horse (ʻUqāb), his daughter (ar-Rabāb) and his granddaughter (Susanna). Immediately after this the marvellous reappears in two contrasting forms: first with the surprising appearance of a robust gazelle adorned with draperies and jewels, and seeming to be a good omen for happy adventures; then with the macabre discovery of a huge skull which presages sad events.

It is in the second part (fol. 32b-36b) that the marvellous is given greatest space, with the miracle of the tree which restores health and youth, and the affair of the Princess ar-Rabab, virgin mother destined to die prematurely.

The third and longest part (fol. 36b-44a) is characterised by a more serious but no less attractive narration: it turns on the story of Susanna and the attempt of the two old hermits Hiram and Huraym to do violence to her.

The few lines of the conclusion (fol. 44b) hint at the unforeseen and irreversible choice which the king finally makes, after watching, disconcerted and astonished, as one extraordinary event succeeded another.

The whole tale is set in a distant, timeless world, where men live as long as the patriarchs did before the flood. It is the world-gone-by of the 'Israelites' (*Banū Isrā'īl*). It should be made clear that this term does not necessarily designate only the Hebrews of the Bible and their descendants of the pre-Islamic era. The Koran and the Maxims of the Prophet also use it as an undifferentiated name for the Jewish and Christian contemporaries of Mohammed. The most noteworthy image evoked by this word in ancient Islamic literature is religious piety and devout practice. Those, in fact, who consecrated themselves to the cult of God and to asceticism were said to be like the 'Israelites'.[1]

The succession of marvels which take place at such an urgent pace before the king's eyes follows a clear, consistent pattern. The magnificent gazelle which draws the king away from his fel-

---

and Accad (*Genesis* 10:9-12); the first king to have his portrait painted in hunting attire was Ashurnasirpal II (883-859 BC), on the reliefs of his palace in Kalakh.

[1] Cf. *E.I.*², I, 1960, 1051-1053, under the entry *Banū Isrā'īl* by S.D. Goiten. The episode of Susanna is set within a framework of clearly Christian flavour: 1) a sort of sanctuary with hanging lamps, candles, incense and votive offerings; 2) large numbers of servants of God (*i.e.* monks) and ascetics (*i.e.* anchorites) who live in monasteries and isolated cells; 3) the recitation of the Psalms.

years earlier he had disposed of the child because she was born in an unheard-of manner.[1]

4.2 *The 'gardener king' and the Tree of Life (fol. 32a-36b)*

After the preamble of the hunt and the adventure with the marvellous gazelle, the narrator takes us into the heart of the story with a section dominated by the motif of the Tree of Life,[2] an image no less archetypal than those we have already seen, the 'hunter king' and the animal guide. The huge skull found in the cave, which provokes so many doubts about the dogma of resurrection, produces the miraculous tree which springs up in the king's garden.

We shall presently see (§ 5.3) that the theme of the skull has greater importance in the narrative structure of the novella than might at first seem to be the case. However, I am not aware that any other example has been found so far in Arab narrative of a buried skull from which springs a tree whose fruits can restore health and youth, and make a virgin pregnant. This motif therefore deserves close attention. Moreover, it documents the persistence on the cultural horizon of medieval Islam of an ancestral, and virtually universal, belief that the head, or rather the brain, is the seat of the reproductive function.[3] It is no mere chance that Greek mythology narrates that Athena sprang from the head of Zeus: it was always believed that seminal fluid was secreted by the brain, came down the marrow of the spinal column and reached the male genital organ by way of a special duct.[4]

The motif of the buried skull from which springs a miraculous tree is firmly rooted in Oriental Christian culture, where the biblical theme of the Tree of Life soon gave way to the *Legend of*

---

[1] Cf. Le Roux de Lincy *Légendes*, 27-28; Graf *Miti*, 140, note 35.

[2] The Tree of Life is mentioned in the first and in the last books of the Christian Bible: *Genesis* 2:9 and 3:22; *Apocalypse* 22:2, 14 and 19. On the general theme of the Tree of Life, see Lechler *The Tree of Life*, Iacobini *L'albero della vita*, and Ringbom *Paradisus*, 95-98.

[3] On this point, see La Barre *Muelos*, and Grottanelli *Aspetti del sacrificio*, 127.

[4] This conviction is reflected in the sagittal sections of the human body drawn by Leonardo da Vinci in his *Anatomy Notebooks* (Royal Library, Windsor castle, 19097v, III, 3v., drawing reproduced in La Barre, *op. cit.*, cover illustration, explanation on p. 3).

the Wood of the Cross. This legend arises from an episode in the lives of Adam and Eve, narrated in some apocryphal texts such as the *Apocalypse of Moses*,[1] the *Lives of Adam and Eve*[2] and the *Gospel of Nicodemus*.[3]

These ancient texts relate that when Adam reached the end of his days, he charged Seth, his favourite son, to procure a miraculous oil which flows from the Tree of Life in the earthly Paradise. Adam was sure that, if he were anointed with this oil, he would be healed of the sickness which was going to kill him three days later. The archangel Michael did nothing to prevent Seth from entering Eden, but refused to give him the oil, because his father's death was by now imminent. However, he promised that Adam would receive a sacred oil from the hands of Christ the Redeemer.[4]

From this shared premise two different versions of the *Legend of the Wood of the Cross* arose, though they also share the characteristic of regarding the place of Adam's burial as the umbilicus of the world, the axis around which the whole of sacred history revolves.[5]

---

[1] Cf. Rosso Ubigli *Apocalisse di Mosè*, 421, 423-424, §§ ix and xiii (reprint: 583, 585-586).

[2] Cf. Rosso Ubigli *Vita di Adamo ed Eva*, 462-463, §§ xxxvi and xli (reprint: 624-625); Bertrand *La vie grecque d'Adam et Eve*, 75, § ix, 3; 77-79, § xiii, 2; 118-119.

[3] Cf. Craveri *Vangeli apocrifi*, 353, 360, 372: *Vangelo di Nicodemo*, Greek text ch. xix, Latin text A ch. xix, Latin text B ch. xx.

[4] Cf. Delumeau *Storia del Paradiso*, 68 and 71. This episode shows how Seth was considered an exceptional figure, able to receive angelic messages and communicate them to others, and to be informed of the divine mysteries, cf. Bertrand, *La vie grecque d'Adam et Eve*, 59-60. According to the gnostic version of the same episode, which survives in the literature of the Mandaeans, the chaste Seth, "leaving his body of flesh and blood and putting on a splendid robe and a sublime, pure turban of light", ascended to heaven in a great shining cloud and there interceded with the "First Great Life" that his father should receive the gift of knowledge, cf. Lupieri *Mandei*, 71-72, 222-223 (*Ginza Smala* I,I); Albrile *Sethiani*, 378. This gift permitted Adam to face death serenely, though previously it had terrified him. From that moment Seth became the intermediary between the divinity and human beings, and the vehicle of soteriological revelation.

[5] The motif of Adam's tomb as the umbilicus of the world is extensively developed in the *Cave of Treasures*, a 6th-century Syriac work

In the first version, the archangel gives Seth a branch with three leaves taken from the Tree of Original Sin (in fact the Tree of the Knowledge of Good and Evil and the Tree of Life, which are quite distinct in the Bible,[1] here coincide), and tells him to plant it on his father's grave.[2] According to the second version, Seth was given three seeds from the tree, and told to put them under Adam's tongue before he was buried. In both versions three shoots spring from the grave of Adam and grow into a single great tree, to be seen, at one and the same time, as a cedar – symbol of the Father; a cypress – symbol of the Son; and a pine – symbol of the Holy Spirit. From the essence of these three trees the Holy Cross was made.

Given the religious significance of the subject, the *Legend of the Wood of the Cross* had extraordinary success in Western European medieval literature too. It was reproduced not only in Latin,[3] but, from the 12th century, in all the vernaculars, from Provençal[4] to Swedish[5] and Icelandic.[6] The most famous pictorial representation of the legend is the fresco of the *Death of Adam*, painted at Arezzo in 1452 by Piero della Francesca. It occupies the

---

which was translated into Arabic, cf. Battista-Bagatti *Caverna dei Tesori*; Su-Min Ri *Caverne des Trésors*. Under the name of "Cave of Treasures" a Jewish tradition identified a cave on Mount Moriah where Adam and Eve were supposed to have taken refuge and to have been buried. In Christian times, between 70 AD and the middle of the 2nd century, this cave was symbolically transferred to Mount Golgotha. On the role of Golgotha as axis of the world, see also Ringbom *Paradisus*.

[1] Cf. *Genesis* 2:9 and 3:22.

[2] In a Persian tradition regarding the *Ṣanoubar*, the Iranian Tree of Life, Seth is replaced in his role as planter by Japheth, son of Noah, cf. Scarcia *Çemberlitaş, Monodendron, Ṣanoubar*, 309-310.

[3] Mussafia *Sulla leggenda* and Meyer *Geschichte* quote Geoffrey of Viterbo (*Pantheon* XIV), Jacob of Varagine (*Legenda Aurea: De inventione sanctae crucis* LXVIII), Gervais of Tilbury (*Otia imperialia*) and other medieval Latin authors who report the legend. Seth's mission in Heaven is narrated in a fragment interpolated in the *Tesoro* of Brunetto Latini published as an appendix by Mussafia *Sulla leggenda*.

[4] Cf. Graf *Leggenda*.

[5] Cf. Mussafia *Sulla leggenda*, 186: *Ett forn-Svenskt legendarium*, edit. Stephens, Stockholm 1858, 89 and 1253.

[6] Cf. Meyer (*Geschichte*, p. 151) quotes the Icelandic *Hanksbók* written by Hankr Erlendsson (d. 1334).

lunette of the right-hand wall of the choir in the church of St Francis.

But even in the Christian tales where the Tree of Life is not explicitly connected with the Wood of the Cross, its origin is always retraced to the Garden of Eden. The anonymous author of the *Search for the Holy Grail* (12th century), for example, tells us that the Tree of Life sprang from the twig on which hung the apple of the first sin. Eve, he says, took it out of Eden and planted it near her home to keep alive the memory of her fatal error.[1]

The Christian motif of the redeeming tree springing from a human skull can also, however, be grafted on to the very ancient theme of the 'gardener king'. This is what happened in the case of the *Story of the skull and the king.*

The theme of the 'gardener king' was studied by Widengren, starting from Sumerian and Akkadian texts and pictorial representations of the third millennium BC, which describe specific religious functions celebrated by the king.[2] Widengren's research shows that the ancient sovereigns of the Syro-Mesopotamian area had the task of guarding a particular temple garden in which, beside a stretch of water, there grew a sacred plant, symbol of the cult of the mystical Tree of Life. The stretch of water in its turn represented the ocean of fresh waters (Sumerian *apzu*, Akkadian *apsû*) in which the Tree of Life had put down its roots.[3] The king was at once the priest for libations of this holy tree and the gardener (Sumerian $^{(\text{lú})}$nu.kiri$_6$, Akkadian *nukarribu*) who watered and pruned it.[4] The king used its branches for magical-medical purifications, and from its fruits extracted an ointment for the body and above all for the head.[5]

In Islamic imagination the cosmic Tree of Life is represented by the immense, wonderful tree called *Ṭūbā*, 'Bliss', which the Prophet Mohammed saw on the occasion of his ascension into

---

[1] Cf. Hucher *Le Saint-Graal*, II, 452-480.

[2] Widengren *The King and the Tree of Life*. The first chapter (5-19) of this short treatise is entitled "The King as a Gardener".

[3] Cf. Widengren *op. cit.*, 6, 19, 64; Ringbom *op. cit.*, 96-97; Delumeau *Storia del Paradiso*, 13. A generous spring of healing paradisiacal water gushes from beneath the threshold of the imaginary temple of Jerusalem prefigured in *Ezekiel* 47:1-12.

[4] Cf. Widengren *op. cit.*, 15, 59.

[5] Cf. Widengren *op. cit.*, 59.

Paradise. The fruits of the *Ṭūbā* taste like ginger mixed with honey, and at its base spring up fountains of wine which flows in rivers throughout Paradise.[1]

The ancient motifs of the 'gardener king' and the Tree of Life certainly inspired the description given by the anonymous author of the *Story of the skull and the king* of the miraculous plant that springs up in the king's garden (fol. 34a-b). Near this plant the king has a portico built; he lights camphor candles round it, hangs lanterns from its boughs and lays votive offerings at its base. Meanwhile he distributes its fruits to all those in need.

The detail of the building of the portico in the king's garden is not, incidentally, without interest, since a great many representations of the earthly paradise in Sasanian, Palaeochristian, Byzantine and Palaeoislamic art include the iconographic motif of the portico which marks out a sacred area or that of the columns of a circular sanctuary.[2]

Another equally significant detail is the first signs of the withering of the tree when the king's daughter ar-Rabâb becomes pregnant, and its drying up when she dies (fol. 36a-b). This recalls a passage from a little-known Arab-Christian work, *The Struggle of Adam*, which relates that at the moment when Adam and Eve left Eden, the Tree of the Knowledge of Good and Evil turned yellow and dried up.[3]

The themes of the Tree of Life and the 'gardener king', meanwhile, call to mind the short medieval French poem mentioned earlier *à propos* the motif of the hunted cervid (§ 4.1). To the best of my knowledge this is the only text apart from our novella which attributes to the Tree of Life the ability to make a virgin pregnant and to cause pregnancies and deliveries which are, to say the least, unusual.

---

[1] Cf. *Libro della Scala di Maometto*, Ch. XXXIX, §§ 99-100, 68-69, and note to page 144. On the motif of the heavenly tree in Neo-Persian literature, see Bausani *Persia religiosa*, 246-249, 337-340.

[2] Cf. Ringbom, *Paradisus*, 166-243 (portico with columns and arches, round or horseshoe-shaped); 243-284 (circular sanctuary with columns and ceiling in the form of a cupola or cone).

[3] Cf. Battista-Bagatti *Combattimento di Adamo*, § 3, 34. Anecdotal text written in Arabic between the 8th and 9th centuries and translated into Ethiopic.

> One thousand years after the sin of Adam and Eve, God transported the Tree of Life to Abraham's garden and an angel prophesied to him that on the wood of that tree the Son of God would be crucified. One of Abraham's daughters was so intoxicated by the scent of the flowers of the tree that she became pregnant. Of course, she was slandered and condemned to be burnt at the stake, but when they set fire to the wood, it turned into a rose tree and the flames turned into birds. When her time came, the girl gave birth to a baby boy, who was given the name of Fanuel.[1] He became king and emperor and, as keeper of the Tree of Life, gave its fruits to the sick who hastened from all sides to be healed. One day Fanuel absentmindedly dried the knife he had just used to cut a fruit on his thigh. From that very moment the thigh became horribly swollen and the doctors and wise men of the kingdom were consulted in vain. After nine months a baby girl was born of Fanuel's thigh. Flabbergasted at becoming a father in this unheard-of fashion, he turned her over to one of his servants to be disposed of in the forest. But a dove told the man that of this child a virgin would be born in whom God would take on flesh and blood, so he laid her in a swans' nest. There, for ten whole years, she was fed by a wonderful doe whose antlers were covered with all kinds of flowers. One day Fanuel, out hunting with his steward Joachim, came upon this stupendous doe. Following her, he wounded her and found her by the girl's nest. She recognised her father and begged him to spare the life of the animal that had nurtured her. Astonished and overjoyed, Fanuel took her to the palace and gave her in marriage to Joachim. The girl was St Anne, future mother of the Virgin Mary.

This remarkable tale forms the prologue to the *Romanz de Saint Fanuel et de Sainte Anne et de Nostre Dame et de Nostre Segnor et de ses Apostres*, a *fabliau* or minstrel composition on a religious subject, from the 13th century.[2] The verse tale of the Emperor Fanuel was published for the first time, though only in

---

[1] The Hebrew name Fanuel 'face of God' corresponds to the name of the father of the prophetess Anna, the 80-year-old Jerusalem widow mentioned in *Luke* 2:36 in the description of the presentation of the child Jesus at the Temple. It is evident that a popular tradition has identified this figure with St. Anne, mother of the Virgin Mary, thus making Fanuel the maternal great-grandfather of Jesus.

[2] Cf. Arcangeli Marenzi *Tema della Vergine*, 33. Gianni Mombello (*Noël du Séminaire d'Aoste*, 173, 178-179) has recently found an allusion to the *Romanz de Fanuel* in a little Christmas poem from the Aosta Valley, dating from the beginning of the 16th century.

part, in 1836 by Le Roux de Lincy,[1] a French man of letters who had found it in a verse codex by Herman de Valenciennes.[2] In 1885 and 1888 Chabaneau published the entire romance, basing his edition on a manuscript in the library of the Montpellier School of Medicine (13th-14th century).[3] Other manuscripts which include this composition were described by Paul Meyer in 1887 and in 1896.[4]

Critics have tried in vain to identify the original source of this bizarre, fantastic composition, defined as a 'curious sample of pseudo-literature'.[5] All, however, have assumed exotic ancestry: 'il a toute l'apparence et la couleur d'un conte oriental'.[6] Now, with the discovery of the *Story of the skull and the king*, we are in a position to point to a probable antecedent. Both the French poem and the Arab novella tell substantially the same story, involving several generations: Abraham, his daughter, his grandson Fanuel and Fanuel's daughter St. Anne in the one case; the king, his daughter ar-Rabâb and his granddaughter Susanna on the other.

There are numerous narrative themes which the *Romanz de Saint Fanuel* shares with the *Story of the skull and the king*, though the approach is different:

A - The miraculous tree which springs up in the garden.

B - The 'gardener king' and the sick people who come to him to be healed.

C - The virgin conceptions brought about by a vegetable agent and the abnormal deliveries: from the father's thigh or the mother's right side.

D - The slanderers and the sentence of death by burning.

E - The assembly of scholars and wise men.

---

[1] Le Roux de Lincy Légendes, 24-27.

[2] Cf. *Histoire littéraire de la France*, XVIII, 833-837.

[3] Cf. Chabaneau *Romanz de Saint Fanuel.*

[4] Cf. Meyer *Notice*. There is a subtle critical analysis of the *Romanz de Saint Fanuel* in Arcangeli Marenzi *op. cit.*, 26-47. In 1977 this poem was the subject of a thesis at the University of Chicago: William Musil, *Le Roman de Saint Fanuel: édition critique* (*Dissertation Abstracts. A. The humanities and social sciences*, Ann Arbor, 38 (1977-78), No. 1374A.

[5] Cf. Arcangeli Marenzi *Tema della Vergine*, 33, 37.

[6] *Histoire littéraire de la France*, XVIII, 836. Cf. Arcangeli Marenzi *op. cit.*, 34, 36.

F - The hunting and pursuit of a marvellous cervid which leads the king to a meeting foreordained by Providence.

G - The hero who, at the end of the story, arranges a marriage: in one case, Zechariah's son marries a lovely girl; in the other, St. Anne becomes the bride of St Joachim.

In the Arab novella these themes are arranged in a very different order, namely F E A B C D G. Only theme G is in the same position in both texts. However, it may be hypothesised that the *Story of the skull and the king*, which seems to be much earlier than 13th century, offers the original narrative outline and that a medieval French minstrel, hearing a vague echo of the Arab novella, freely rearranged the themes, giving his 'uncontrolled imagination'[1] its head.

As to theme C, the oldest Middle-Eastern text to narrate a pregnancy brought about by a vegetable agent is Egyptian and goes back to the end of the nineteenth dynasty (1320-1200 BC). This is the famous *Tale of two brothers*.[2] A woman who has killed her husband becomes the Pharaoh's favourite, but senses the mysterious presence of her husband in two gigantic avocado plants growing on either side of the palace gates. The woman beseeches the Pharaoh to have them cut down, saying that she wants to use the wood to make furniture. As the workers are hastening to cut down the plants, a splinter flies into the woman's mouth; she swallows it, and thus becomes pregnant. Her son, as an adult, is to cause her downfall.

The motif of the intoxicating scent emanating from the blossoms of the plants in Paradise is to be found in the already-mentioned apocryphal text, *Life of Adam and Eve*.[3]

According to Dumézil,[4] the oldest figurative representations of the miraculous birth of a child from its father's thigh (as Anne is born from Fanuel's thigh) may be found on a gold vase (12th-11th century BC) found at Hasanlu, in Persian Azerbaijan, and on a bronze votive offering in Luristan (8th-7th century BC; § 1.2.3).[5] The Indo-European myth pictured there is of the birth of a

---

[1] The phrase is quoted from Arcangeli Marenzi *op. cit.*, 45.

[2] Cf. Saintyves *Vierges Mères*, Ch. III, 64-66; Bresciani *Antico Egitto*, 376-385.

[3] Cf. Bertrand *La vie grecque d'Adam et Eve*, 101, § xxxviii, 4; 141.

[4] Dumézil *Roman des jumeaux*, 97-99.

[5] Cf. Dussaud *Anciens bronzes*, 196-229, especially 205-206, No. 5,

hero whose foetus is extracted from the mother's womb and transplanted in his father's thigh. In India, this myth is reflected in the birth of Aurva ('thigh'), son of Cyavana and of Arushī;[1] in Greece, in the birth of Dionysus, son of Zeus and Semele.[2] These distant links with the story of Fanuel were pointed out by Arturo Graf in 1892.[3] The only mythic example of birth from a mother's side, so far as I know, is that of Siddhârtha Gautama, known as the Buddha. It is said that Queen Mâyâ gave birth to him from her right side and that she died a few days later.[4] It is truly remarkable that the Indian queen and Princess ar-Rabâb, mother of Susanna, should be united by the same destiny.

4.3 *The affair of Susanna, the young anchorite (fol. 36b-44a)*

The episode of the young anchorite who is slandered and whose name is then cleared poses one of the most intriguing problems of the *Story of the skull and the king*. It is not – as at first sight it may seem – a reworking of the biblical tale of Susanna, but, strange as it may seem, a fairly faithful reproduction of the Samaritan variant of this tale. It is, however, greatly to be wondered at that an Arabian Muslim narrator should be inspired by Samaritan literature, one of the most marginal and least accessible of Near-East literatures. On the other hand it seems reasonable to suppose that the Samaritans took over a transformation of *Susanna* circulating in other environments, adapting it to their own religion and culture.

4.3.1 *The Samaritan 'Susanna'*

No fewer than three versions of the Samaritan variant of the tale of Susanna survive:

1 - a major version (G), rich in detail, in the *Book of Joshua*, a Samaritan text in Hebrew published in 1908 by Gaster;[5]

Fig. 7.

[1] Cf. *Mahābhārata*, Book III, chs. 169-171; Monier-Williams *Sanskrit Dictionary*, 239.

[2] Cf. Chirassi Colombo *Gravidanze maschili.*

[3] Graf *Miti*, 140, note 35.

[4] Cf. Auboyer-Nou *Buddha*, 18-20; Tab. 3, 32.

[5] Gaster *Daughter of Amram*, 201-206. This is a text in Samaritan

2 - an intermediate version (AF), in the Samaritan chronicle in Arabic by Abū l-Fatḥ, published by Vilmar in 1865;[1]

and lastly,

3 - a minor version (AS), a brief summary of Gaster's text, in the Samaritan chronicle in Hebrew published by Adler and Seligsohn in 1903.[2]

Collating the three, the story they tell, briefly, is this:

> The high priest Amram had a beautiful, devout and studious daughter who had copied the Torah with her own hand. Her name is not recorded. One day she asked her father's permission to serve the Lord for a whole year as a Nazirite on the holy mountain Gerizim. Her father agreed, and had a dwelling built for her a little way below the summit of the mountain, not far from where two Nazirites had been living in isolation for 25 years. These two, seeing her reciting the Psalms and reading the Torah by moonlight on the terrace above her dwelling, fell madly in love with her, for her face shone more than the very moon. So they decided to approach her with a trick and laid their hands on her. At first the girl tried to resist, then she put a good face on it and asked them to give her the time to perfume herself and put on her best clothes, saying that they could do as they wished with her. She even made them believe that her lust was greater than theirs. Going back to her dwelling, she barricaded herself inside and addressed a long, heartfelt plea to the Lord. God intervened, making the two hermits temporarily blind so that they could not find her door.[3] Furiously angry, they went down to Sichem, where the population welcomed them, astonished and excited, for they had not been seen for 25 years. Before the high priest and the whole congregation in the synagogue they announced that they had seen the girl fornicating with a stranger. While the Samaritans were assembling in an open space to watch the girl being burned at the stake,[4] her father, weeping, was ap-

Hebrew, deriving from a 15th-century codex written in Arabic.

[1] The *Kitāb at-Tārīkh* by Abū l-Fatḥ dates back to the 14th century, cf. Vilmar *Abū l-Fatḥ*; Stenhouse *Falasha and Samaritan versions*.

[2] Adler-Seligsohn *Chronique samaritaine*, 42-44. Reprinted in a German translation by M.J. Bin Gorion in his book *Born Judas*, Leipzig 1916, I, 45-46.

[3] Cf. *Genesis* 19:11. In the AS version there is no mention of the momentary blindness of the hermits.

[4] The young woman was condemned to the pyre on the basis of the

proaching, coming through the vineyards with his town-crier.[1] There they saw a group of angels, disguised as Samaritan children playing at court cases.[2] The boy who was acting the part of the high priest was busy questioning the two who were taking the roles of the Nazirites, one after the other separately. Learning his lesson, Amram the high priest hastened to apply it to the real Nazirites, and so discovered that their testimonies did not coincide. Once their guilt had been proved, the false witnesses were condemned to death. According to G they were first stoned, then thrown into the fire;[3] according to AF they were only stoned,[4] while in AS, in conformity with the law, they were burned at the stake.[5] Amram's daughter was then welcomed into the city with great celebrations.

The Samaritan legend offers an original reworking of two themes which must have been present even before the Falasha variant (§ 1.3). The first of these is the theme of the young woman who dedicates herself body and soul to the service of the Lord. As we have seen, this is also the case with the protagonist of the Judaeo-Ethiopian tale. The second is the theme of angelic assistance, which in the Falasha tale comes from the archangel Michael.

Now, it is more likely that the figure of the young widow who needs solitude and prayer inspired the motif of the virgin who lives alone in a hermitage, than vice versa. Similarly, it is more probable that an angelic rescuer was transformed into a close-knit band of angel-children playing at court cases, than the other way about. I do not believe that the information about the angelic nature of these children, found only in the Samaritan G version, is a late, secondary detail. This version, in suggesting that a double penalty was inflicted on the two culprits (stoning and the stake), also shows that it is following the same narrative line as the

---

precept in *Leviticus* 21:9, regarding the sanctity of the priesthood.

[1] The detail of crossing the vineyards is missing from the AF and AS versions.

[2] According to the AF version, the boys whom the high priest came upon were simply sons of Samaritans, cf. Stenhouse *Falasha and Samaritan versions*, 98. The episode is ignored by the AS version.

[3] Cf. *Deuteronomy* 19:19.

[4] Cf. Stenhouse *ibidem*, 98.

[5] Cf. Adler-Seligsohn *Chronique samaritaine*, 44.

Septuagint, where we are told that they were thrown into a ravine to be stoned[1] and that the Angel of the Lord then burned them with a lightning bolt.[2] The theme of fire as a penalty is also present in AS, whereas Abū l-Fatḥ's version (AF), which mentions only stoning, prefers to follow Theodotion's 2nd-century AD version.

It is not possible to say when the Samaritan variant of the tale of Susanna took form, but there is an important clue in favour of its relative antiquity. This is the episode already mentioned in the *Story of David* (§ 2.3), which goes back to the end of the 7th or beginning of the 8th century AD. There for the first time we come upon the group of adolescents whom the slandered girl's grandfather meets by chance, and from whom emerges the boy who is destined to become a famous man. This figure is missing from the Samaritan variant of *Susanna*. The young Solomon, in the *Story of David*, so sensible and so enterprising, is not, however, given charge of the trial. This role falls to King David in person, as in the Samaritan version it falls to the high priest Amram. Moreover, the *Story of David* seems to document the penultimate phase of a motif which was to culminate only with the *Story of the skull and the king* in the triumph of one of the boys, as a worthy emulator of the prophet David.

Going back to the *Story of the skull and the king*, it is striking how closely the Arabian episode of Susanna corresponds to the Samaritan one. The following list shows how many important points of contact there are between the two texts:

1) a virgin, daughter or granddaughter of the leading authority of the place, wishes to consecrate herself to God and asks her father/grandfather to build her a cell in a secluded place. Here, day and night, she recites the Psalms and praises the Lord.

2) Two ascetics who live nearby lust after her and plot to rape her with a trick.

3) The girl shows how astute she is by pretending to cooperate, and escaping them by barricading herself in her cell.

---

[1] Cf. Stenhouse *Falasha and Samaritan versions*, 99.

[2] Wurmbrand (*Falasha Susanna*, note 3, 34-35) is of the conflicting opinion that the double penalty imposed on the hermits in the G version is proof that the text published by Gaster is late, and composite.

4) The two ascetics, feeling that she has made fools of them, decide to divert the scandal, accusing the girl of fornication with a stranger.

5) The population of the city are greatly surprised at their arrival.

6) The virgin is condemned to be burnt alive and a pyre is built in a great square.

7) The father/grandfather withdraws, before the execution, to a place where he can find comfort, and unexpectedly sees the game of court cases played by children. The witnesses are questioned separately on their accusations against the consecrated girl, but their testimonies differ.

8) The false witnesses, condemned to death, are first stoned, then burned on the pyre (cf. the Septuagint version of the tale of Susanna).

How and where the author of the *Story of the skull and the king* came to know the Samaritan variant remains an extremely interesting question. Our text may be a further clue to the influence which, according to authoritative scholars, Samaritan culture exercised on Islam in the first two centuries. It is thought, in fact, that Islam drew important elements of its final identity from Samaritanism in order to make as clear as possible its distinction from Judaism and Christianity.[1] The encounter with the ideological and ritual Samaritan heritage should have occurred, therefore, in the Umayyad era (661-750 AD), certainly before the Maxims of the Prophet, Islamic law and Koranic exegesis were committed to writing. This process of codification began only about the year 143 of the Hegira (760-761 AD).[2]

On the other hand, however, the *Story of the skull and the king* also converges with the Falasha variant of the tale of Susanna in two details of no small importance. First, the consecrated virgin is called 'Susanna' as in the biblical tale and the Falasha version. Secondly, the second question put by the young leader of the faggot-gatherers to the two ascetics coincides with the question

---

[1] On the numerous parallelisms in institutional terms between Samaritanism and Islam, see Moses Gaster, "Samaritaner" in *E.I.*[1], IV, 1934, 132-138; Crone-Cook *Hagarism*, ch. 4, "The Samaritan calques", 21-28; Macuch *Vorgeschichte der Bekenntnisformel*. Noja Noseda (under "al-Sāmira" in *E.I.*[2], VIII, 1995, 1080-1082) suggests that such evaluations should be made cautiously.

[2] Cf. Khoury *Codification*, 110-111.

which, in the Falasha variant, is put to the three elders of the people (§ 1.3): it regards the time at which the witnesses claim to have seen the misdeed.

4.3.2 *Relationships among the various forms of the tale of Susanna*

It is possible, in the context of the possible antecedents and variants of the biblical tale of Susanna, to distinguish a process of evolution in five stages and with various ramifications. The first stage (A), the most distant in time, is that of the myth of Sukanyā and the Heavenly Twins (§ 1.2.3); the second (B) consists of a popular Iranian tale from which derive, on the one hand, the Islamic legend of Hārūt and Mārūt (B.1; § 1.2.2) and, on the other, the Jewish legend of Shamḥazay and 'Aza'el (B2; § 1.2.1).

In A as in B, the motifs of the 'lovely slandered woman' and the 'wise young man' are still absent. In A and B, the whole affair involves only three characters: a young married woman, and two supernatural beings. In B2 the number falls even lower, to two: an 'angelic watcher' and a virgin. In contrast with A, the B stage shows the supernatural being's passion for a woman being severely punished.

The third stage (C) is represented by the archetype from which branch off, on the one hand, the biblical tale (C1; § 1.1), on the other the ultimate source of the Falasha variant, which we know only thanks to a 15th-century manuscript (C2; § 1.3). This phase is characterised by the substitution of two or more men of authority for the two angels: in the biblical tale there are two, in the Judaeo-Ethiopian tale there are three. At the same time there comes into play the motif of the 'lovely slandered woman', which in its turn involves the entrance on the scene of a positive angelic figure, almost as though to compensate for the replacement of the Watchers with human beings. Hence the 'Angel of the Lord' in the biblical tale, identified, of course, in the Falasha tale with the Archangel Michael. Whereas in the Judaeo-Ethiopian tale Michael acts personally in human disguise, in the Septuagint version he delegates the young Daniel, remaining behind the scenes, but at the end he intervenes directly, annihilating the two culprits. In Theodotion's Greek version, the angel is excluded: he has become an inconvenient figure. Daniel is thus transformed from a mere executor of the angel's commands to the real protagonist of the story.

The Arabian version of the *Tazyīn al-aswāq* (16th century) is linked to the medieval transmission of the Greek Septuagint source; the Hebrew version handed down by Jerahmeel ben Solomon (12th century, § 2.1) also refers to it. The episode cited in the *Thousand and One Nights* (§ 2.2) seems rather to go all the way back to the Semitic (Hebrew or Aramaic) origin of the tale of Susanna.

Both the biblical (C1) and the Falasha (C2) tales still in a sense belong to the genre of sacred history, the former thanks to the figure of Daniel, the latter because of the role played by the Archangel Michael. In complete contrast, the further developments of the tale of Susanna are either pious tales or didactic novellas.

In the fourth stage (D) the heroine is transformed from a young wife to a young woman who has no intention of marrying. The Samaritan 'Susanna' (D1; § 4.3.1) and the 'Susanna' of the *Story of David* (D2; § 2.3) have a common source of this nature. This phase of development is closer to the Falasha tale than to the biblical version. There is no longer any hint at the figure of Daniel, the 'wise young man' delegated by the 'Angel of the Lord'. He is replaced, at least in the Samaritan variant handed down to us in the Samaritan *Book of Joshua*, by a small group of angels, who, disguised as urchins playing at court cases, teach the high priest how to question and punish his daughter's slanderers. In the Samaritan versions of the chronicle of Abū l-Fatḥ and of the chronicle published by Adler and Seligsohn, the 'wise young men' are presented as mere children. Their angelic nature is no longer considered important. In the corresponding episode of the *Story of David* it is the young Solomon and his playmates who fulfil this role.

The fifth and last stage (E) of the evolutionary process regarding our tale is represented by the affair of Susanna in the *Story of the skull and the king* (§ 3: fol. 36b-44a). This seems to depend directly on the Samaritan variant of the tale of Susanna (D1), but also includes the theme of the young prophet (the young Solomon of the *Story of David*, D2) who plays at presiding over a debate in court. What is original in the author of our novella is the partial inclusion of the legend in the context of the biblical tale. On the one hand he recovers the original name of the protagonist, which was recalled only in the Falasha variant; on the other, he restores to the most brilliant of the young succourers, in the person of the son of the prophet Zechariah, the role of actual judge of the false witnesses – a role which, in the Bible, was assigned to Daniel.

I think it is worth noting that in all its phases, with the exception of the *Story of David*, our tale has been inspired by the Ninth Commandment: 'Thou shalt not covet thy neighbour's wife'.[1] In the Samaritan variant, and in the one included in the *Story of the skull and the king*, this admonition is extended to those who lust after a virgin consecrated to God.

I may summarise the relationships delineated here as follows:

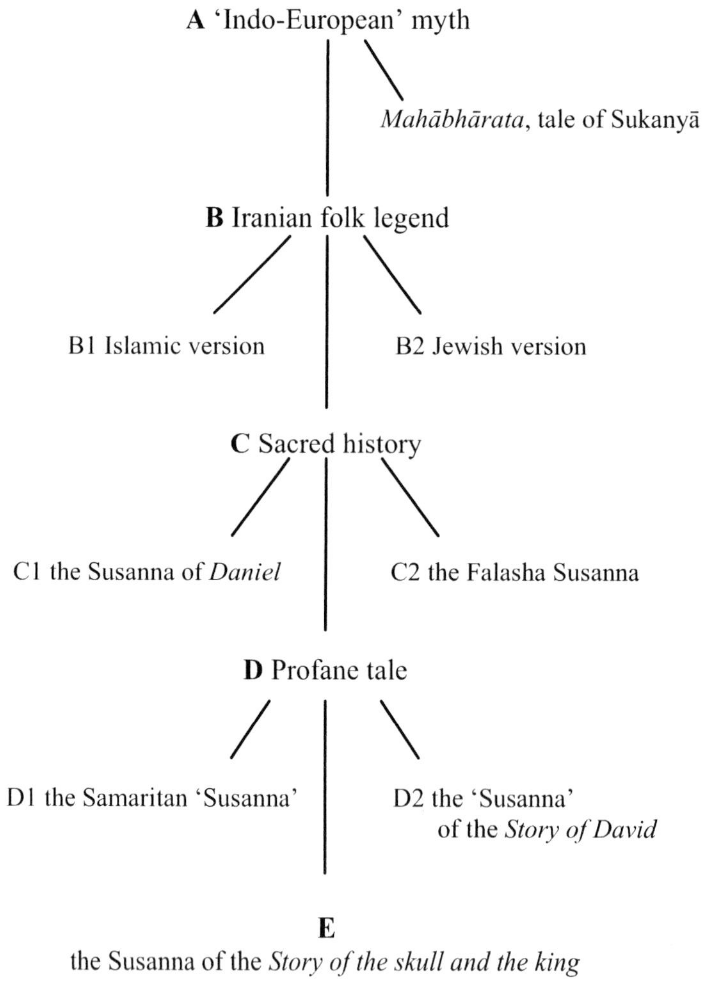

---

[1] *Exodus* 20:17 and *Deuteronomy* 5:21.

Roles:	RELATION	YOUNG WOMAN	WOOERS	DEFENDER
A	*husband*	*young bride*	*2 demigods*	Ø
	Cyavana	Sukanyā	he Heavenly Twins	Ø
B	*(husband)*	*young bride*	*2 angels*	Ø
B1	----	Nāhid	Hārūt and Mārūt	Ø
B2	----	Estera	Shemḥazay	Ø
C	*husband /father*	*young bride*	*2 men (false witnesses)*	*1 angel*
C1	Joakim (husband)	Susanna	2 elders of the people	+ (1 angel +) Daniel
C2	the king (father)	widowed princess	3 elders	the archangel Michael
D		*young unmarried woman*	*2/4 men (false witnesses)*	*+ group of angels/boys playing at court cases*
D1	Amram (father)	young Nazirite	2 Nazirites	group of angels/boys
D2	-----	young unmarried woman	4 high dignitaries	+ group of boys
E	*the king (grandfather)*	*young female hermit*	*2 ascetics (false witnesses)*	*group of boys one of whom plays the judge*

4.3.3 *A possible parallel in medieval Italian literature*

The narrative line inaugurated by the Samaritan ‘Susanna’ and by the Susanna of the *Story of the skull and the king,* consecrated virgins who are isolated in a secluded cell but do not escape the attentions of two lustful and unscrupulous old men, seems not to have died out on the eastern and southern shores of the Mediterranean. Indeed, it may have crossed the sea to live again in the west in one of the stories in the *Decameron.*

This is the tenth story of the third day, the most coldly obscene that Boccaccio ever wrote. The heroine is a fourteen-year-old Muslim virgin with the exotic name of Alibech,[1] who ardently longs to serve God in the Thebaid desert. As the heading has it, ‘Alibech becomes a recluse and a monk named

[1] In medieval Turkish Alibech (*Ali bek*) meant ‘Mr. Ali’.

Rustico teaches her how to put the Devil back into hell. Then, she is led away from there to become the wife of Neerbal'.[1]

Vittore Branca observes that the antecedents of this novella are 'few and very vague, not to say non-existent'.[2] And in fact the various attempts that have been made to find analogies with other late ancient or medieval narrative texts from western, or at least Christian, cultures have not, thus far, yielded convincing results.[3] It is, however, worth noting a tale which does belong to another cultural horizon, but which nonetheless offers fitting correspondence with the *Decameron* novella.

First of all, the background against which the episode of Susanna begins in the *Story of the skull and the king* is identical to that of Boccaccio's novella: a distant land in which, here and there, are scattered ascetics' cells and monasteries for the servants of God, just like the descriptions of the deserts of Egypt in the *Lives of the holy fathers*. The heroines – one the granddaughter of a king, the other the daughter of a very wealthy man from 'Capsa in Barberia', have just entered puberty but are both stirred by a strong desire to serve God in solitude. In their search for spiritual perfection, they both meet with hermits: Susanna against her will, Alibech in the course of her postulancy. These men, fearful that they will be unable to resist her beauty, entrust her to Rustico, a holy hermit who, younger than they, is reckless and presumptuous.

---

[1] Cf. Boccaccio, Giovanni, *The Decameron. 21 Novelle selected, translated and edited by Mark Musa and Peter E. Bondanella*, New York: W.W. Norton & Company, 1977, pp. 69-73. To make clear the terms of the metaphor is sufficient a short quotation of the dialogue between Alibech and Rustico (pp. 70.71): "'Rustico, what is that thing I see sticking out in front of you and which I do not possess?. Oh, my child' replied Rustico 'that is the Devil, about whom I told you. Now you can see him for yourself. He is inflicting such pain on me that I can hardly bear it'. 'God be praised!' said the girl 'I am better off than you are, for I do not possess this Devil'. 'That is very true' Rustico replied 'but you have something else I do not have, and you have it in place of this'. 'Oh!' answered Alibech 'What is it?'. 'possess hell' said Rustico 'and I firmly believe that God has sent you here for the salvation of my soul'".

[2] Cf. Branca *Decameron*, 443, note 1.

[3] See, for example, Alfonso Paolella's attempt (Paolella *Rustico ed Alibech*) to establish a structural analogy between the novella of Alibech and the life of St. Mary the Egyptian. Cf. Migiel *Beyond seduction*, 171.

From this point the two novellas take very different narrative lines. Susanna, overcoming her initial disconcertment, reacts with great presence of mind and escapes from her tempters with unexpected guile, by giving them the clear impression that her one thought is to do as they wish. Alibech reacts quite differently, submitting to Rustico with passive, provocative naiveté.

It is reasonable to suppose at this point that Boccaccio may have heard some echo of the Susanna section of the *Story of the skull and the king*, when he was undergoing his human and intellectual formation in Neaples (1328-1340). At the time of Robert d'Anjou (1309-1343), Neaples was a magnificent metropolis and a leading trade centre in which men, goods and ideas converged from all the Mediterranean countries, especially North Africa.[1]

Thus the Arabian novella may somehow have crossed the sea. It is in any case apparent from the *Romanz de Saint Fanuel* (13th century, § 4.2) that a tradition parallel to another section of the *Story of the skull and the king* had already been known in Europe for some time. From this perspective, in utterly transforming the cunning chastity of the heroine of a cautionary Arab tale into the unwitting provocativeness of Alibech, Boccaccio may be offering a further mocking parody of motifs from the monastic tradition and the penitential culture of his time.[2]

5 Epilogue

5.1 *The identity of the young judge*

As one gradually approaches the conclusion of the *Story of the skull and the king*, the essential cruces of the tale come to light. One of these is the identity of the youth charged by the king with questioning and judging the false witnesses Hiram and Huraym. We learn to our surprise (fol. 44a) that he is the son of the prophet Zechariah;[3] and that means he can only be John the Baptist.[1]

---

[1] Cf. Branca *Decameron*, xlii; idem *Boccaccio medievale*, 148. The city of Tunis is mentioned in novellas IV,4 and V,2.

[2] Delcorno *Modelli agiografici*, 350-358.

[3] Zechariah is a New Testament figure greatly venerated by Muslims, who accompany his name, as in our text, with the customary eulogy given by right to a prophet-forerunner of Mohammed: "Peace be upon him!". Zechariah is mentioned in four different chapters (suras) of the

How, then, are we to explain the unexpected appearance of St. John as Daniel's counterpart in the guise of a wise, enlightened boy? A preliminary answer may be suggested by the Koran itself. In the *Sura of Mary* (*Koran* xix, 12) it is written of the Baptist: 'We gave him wisdom from boyhood'. Of no other prophet but Jesus does the Koran say that he was wise in adolescence. In addition, there is an Islamic tradition according to which St. John and Daniel were contemporaries. John is supposed to have suffered a martyr's death at the hands of the Israelites (*Banū Isrā'īl*) in the time of Nebuchadnezzar.[2]

In any case, I believe that John the Baptist's sudden entrance reflects the author's adherence to the ideals and tendencies of the Islamic mystics of the earliest centuries, who – particularly the so-called *bukkā'* (moaners)[3] – were in complete accord with the Christian mystics of Syria and Iraq, and with the spiritual guides of baptism-centred sects.[4] They shared the ideal of poverty and mercy, the lively awareness of sin, the strict practice of abstinence and their devotion to St. John the Baptist, unparalleled model of continence and austerity of life.

When the identity of the young judge is revealed, certain facets of the *Story of the skull and the king* which would otherwise have remained obscure acquire new light. I am thinking, in the first place, of the phobia regarding male and female genitality, which emerges in three passages:

1) conception by swallowing a fruit (fol. 35a);

2) the birth of Susanna from the right side of the virgin ar-Rabāb (fol. 36b);

3) Susanna's enthusiasm for having been born without the intervention of a fleshly father (fol. 37a).

Koran: iii, 37-40; vi, 85; xix, 2-11; xxi, 89-90. On the Islamic tradition regarding him, see Khoury *Wahb b. Munabbih*, I, 243-244.

[1] In the *Koran* John (*Yaḥyā*) is mentioned in three different suras: vi, 85; xix, 7, 12-13; xxi, 90.

[2] Cf. de Goeje *Annales at-Tabari*, II, 716-717.

[3] Cf. *E.I.*[2], I, 1960, 988-990: under the entry *Bakkā'*, pl. *bakkā'ūn*, *bukkā'* by F. Meier; Crone-Cook *Hagarism*, 95.

[4] On the sects of baptizers from the 2nd century AD, see Rudolph *Mandäer*, 1, 222-252; under "Elkesai" (G. Strecker) in *Reallexicon für Antike und Christentum*, IV, coll. 1171-1186; and under "Ṣābi'a" (T. Fahd) in *E.I.*[2], VIII, 1994, 694-698, with an exhaustive bibliography.

Finally, I am thinking of the episode of the six young faggot-gatherers bathing in the water near which the king has withdrawn (fol. 41a). Is not the Baptist the most suitable person to preside over an immersion? Indeed, I would suggest that whoever wrote the novella wanted in this way to recover the famous scene of the chaste bride bathing in the garden, unaware that she is being spied on by two old men (*Dan.* 13:15-19). Given the demands of the new script, the author may have constructed another, no less intriguing bathing scene, with a daring and perhaps humorous inversion of roles: the king withdrawing unseen behind a ruin and from there watching the young men strip and bathe. It must be deduced that the author knew not only the Samaritan variant on the tale of Susanna but the biblical version too. And where else would he have learned the name Susanna?

There is, however, an (at least apparent) contradiction: Zechariah's son does not disdain the gorgeous robes which the king gives him, nor does he refuse to marry the lovely girl who is introduced to him (fol. 44a). The author may have thought that the Baptist responded to the call to perfection only in his maturity.

5.2 *The morals of the fable*

Respecting the structure of the didactic novellas of classical Arab literature,[1] the author of the *Story of the skull and the king* inserts three lines of verse directly before the conclusion, as a moral:

> If you want to dig a pit, make sure that it is wide!
> Be indulgent with young people, if they are inexperienced,
> But don't accept excuses from those who have grey-hair!

This metrical proverb clearly does not refer to the whole novella, but only to the episode whose protagonists are the virgin Susanna and the two sinful old men.[2] The topos of the trap into

---

[1] "Poésie et narration sont inséparables dans la culture arabo-islamique", Khoury *Mille et Une Nuits*, 26. It should be noted that the admonitory tales of mediaeval European literatures, too, are introduced or concluded with appropriate proverbs, cf. Branca *Boccaccio medievale*, lvii.

[2] The first of the three lines of the Arab composition contain two recurrences of a root which appears twice in the tale of the execution of Hiram and Huraym: "the crowd... stoned them... and threw them into the *pit* which *had been dug* for Susanna".

which the snarer himself falls is in any case well known in the sapiential literature of the Near East.[1] But here the message is more clearly stated: it is not enough to be careful not to fall into the pit you have dug with your own hands; you must also foresee how you will get out of it, if by some unhappy chance you fall in. Woe to those who find themselves in a blind alley! In the case of a young man, well, it is understandable, but who can accept that adults, with extensive experience, are incapable of evaluating the consequences of their own actions?

Thus far there is nothing more than the ordinary admonition of popular wisdom. But the author adds a second moral, when he refers to Susanna's answer to the king, who had told her of the result of the trial of Hiram and Huraym. Her comment is expressed in a single line, as blunt and unemotional as an aphorism: 'In vain does man exert himself if with God he is not contented' (fol. 44b).

This is a loftier moral, more in line with the Sufi ideals of ascesis and spiritual perfection; a maxim which transcends the episode of Susanna and the elders to extend itself to the novella in its entirety, to the point where it becomes emblematic. With this answer, in fact, the girl also achieves the aim of inviting the king to conversion, and the old sovereign responds: after his granddaughter's death, he retires to her own cell to worship God and expiate his sin of lack of faith.

5.3 *The hero becomes a hermit*

The motif of the hero who becomes a hermit (fol. 44b) is extremely rare in Islamic culture. In marked contrast, in the *chansons de geste*, the *contes pieux* and the Breton romances written in the 12th-13th centuries, innumerable knights end their careers behind the secluded walls of a hermitage.[2] This is why it is surprising that the protagonist of our novella should give up his throne to devote himself to the service of God. The only historical

---

[1] Cf. *Psalm* 7:15: "He (the wicked man) digs a trap, scoops it out,/ but he falls into the snare he made himself"; *Psalm* 9:15: "The nations have fallen into the trap they made,/ their feet caught in the snare they laid"; *Psalm* 57/56:6b: "They dug a pit ahead of me but fell in it themselves"; *Proverbs* 26:27; *Ecclesiastes* 10:8: "He who digs a pit falls into it"; *Ecclesiasticus* 27:26a: "The man who digs a pit falls into it".

[2] Cf. Delcorno *Modelli agiografici*, 342-343.

personage in Islam of whom something similarly wonderful is told is Ibrāhīm bin Adham (§ 4.1), a wandering ascetic of the 8th century, celebrated by generations of Sufis for his generosity and self-denial, which contrasted with the luxury in which he is thought to have lived as a young man. He was said to have reigned over Balkh, near Amu Darya in Khorasan, but to have early given up the throne to lead an austere contemplative life.[1] According to some authors the legend of Ibrāhīm bin Adham is of Buddhist origin, its direct model being the *Romance of Barlaam and Budasaf*, transmitted by the Manichaeans of Central Asia.[2] In addition to Ibrāhīm bin Adham, two famous epic poems[3] from Persian culture present two more crowned heads who withdraw to religious life. The first of these is the mythical King Lohrāsp, who gave up his throne to his son Goshtāsp and isolated himself in prayer in a temple of fire;[4] the second is Eskandarūs (Alexander), son of Alexander the Great and Roxana, who, shortly after succeeding to his father's throne, withdrew to contemplative life in a solitary place.[5]

5.3.1 *The legend of Jesus and the skull*

On a popular level, and among almost all the peoples of the Islamic world, however, a legend was widespread in which the motif of the king who becomes a hermit is combined in a singular manner with the motif of the skull which inspires reflections on the afterlife. This is the legend of *Jesus and the skull*,[6] which narrates that an idolatrous Israelite king became an ascetic after being brought back to life by Christ. Briefly, the story is as follows:

---

[1] Ibrāhīm bin Adham was born in Balkh and died in Syria in 777-778, cf. *E.I.*², III, 1971, 1010-1011; and Farīd ad-Dīn 'Aṭṭār *Tadhkirat al-Awliyā*, 161-187.

[2] Cf. Molé *I mistici musulmani*, 18, 48-49.

[3] The *Shāhnāme* by Ferdousī (c. 932 - c. 1021) and the *Eskandar-nâme* by Neẓāmī of Ganje (1141-1204).

[4] Cf. Bausani *Letteratura neopersiana*, 379.

[5] Cf. Bausani, *op. cit.*, 437. In fact in 310 BC Alexander (*Eskandarūs*) was assassinated together with his mother by Cassandrus, regent in Macedonia.

[6] Cf. Levi Della Vida *Gesù e il teschio*.

> One day, as he was walking with his disciples, Jesus noticed a large human skull which had been calcined by the sun. He decided to restore its voice to it, so that it might explain to the disciples what happens when we die and what hell is like. Marvellously, the skull took on flesh and skin and introduced itself as an Israelite king, a worshipper of the golden calf. It went on to describe the splendid life of the past and the horrible conditions in which it found itself after death. This king had been powerful and had lived in a sumptuous palace, surrounded by innumerable courtiers and a great army. It happened, however, that he fell gravely ill while out hunting. Despite the care of his doctors and the sacrifices offered to his idol, he soon died. At that moment the Angel of Death seized him and handed him over to two angelic inquisitors. After some time spent alone in the tomb, his soul was thrown into one of the circles of Hell where atrocious torments awaited it. Questioned further by Jesus, the skull described the seven circles of Hell and the types of sinners destined to each. Finally the skull asked Christ to have mercy and save it. Jesus, moved by its appeal, prayed to God and with his assent he restored it entirely to life. From the skull rose a strong, vigorous man who at once professed his faith in the one God of Abraham, Moses and Jesus, and in the future Prophet Mohammed. He then withdrew on to a mountain, where he led an ascetic life to expiate his sin until death.

Like the *Story of the skull and the king*, the legend of *Jesus and the skull* belongs to the popular literary genre of the *Isrā'īlīyât* ('Israelite matters'), *i.e.* the pious tales on the *Banū Isrā'īl* ('the sons of Israel'), as the pre-Islamic monotheists were called.[1] These are tales connected with the activity of the popular exegetes of the Koran, the so-called *quṣṣāṣ* ('narrators'),[2] who circulated them under the names of the best-known traditionalists of the 1st century of the Hegira, especially the Yemenite scholars Ka'b al-Aḥbār and Wahb bin Munabbih. Indeed, various editions of the

[1] Cf. Tottoli *Origin*. On the probable Christian hagiographic sources of the tale of *Jesus and the skull*, see Pennacchietti *San Giorgio* and idem *Il racconto di Giomgiomé*.

[2] On the role of the *quṣṣāṣ* in Islamic literature and in the cultural history of the first centuries of Islam, see the entry *ḳâṣṣ* by C. Pellat in *E.I.*², IV, 1978, 763-765.

legend of *Jesus and the skull*, in prose and verse, are attributed to these two men.

Our first definite knowledge of this legend goes back to the 11th century, from authors from the two extremes of the Islamic world, Iran and Spain: in the first case, the great traditionalist Abū Nu'aym al-Iṣfahānī (948-1038),[1] and the supreme theologian of Islam, Abū Ḥāmid al-Ghazālī (1056-1111); in the second, Abū Bakr aṭ-Ṭarṭūshī (1059-1126), an Arab-Spanish man of letters from Tortosa.[2]

The testimony of Abū Nu'aym al-Iṣfahānī is especially important because, in the chain of guarantors of transmission of the text, he includes Isḥāq bin Bishr Abū Ḥudhayfa, a traditionalist born in Balkh who lived in Bukhara in central Asia (d. 821). Of this figure we know that he wrote a *Kitāb al-mubtada'* ('Book on the beginning of the world'), *i.e.* a collection of 'Stories of the Prophets'.[3] It may be supposed that the legend of *Jesus and the skull* was part of this work, which dates from the beginning of the 9th century[4] (2nd century of the Hegira).

The legend, spread to almost every corner of the Islamic world by storytellers and more or less official preachers, was especially popular in mystic circles: this was where it was put into poetic form and translated into the various Islamic languages. The first hint at the legend of the damned soul restored to life by Jesus is to be found in the *Elāhī-nāme* (the 'Divine Book'), a work in verse by the famous Persian mystic poet Farīd ad-Dīn 'Aṭṭār (c. 1119 - c. 1220), a native of Nishapur, in Khorasan, where he lived.[5] But a short poem of eighty lines entitled *Jomjome nāme* ('The Book of the skull') is also attributed to this poet.[6] It appears that this is the source of the translations and adaptations in Chagatai Turkish, in Kazakh, in Anatolian Turkish, in Kurdish and in Urdu.[7] A verse composition in Maghribi Arabic on the same

---

[1] Cf. *E.I.*[2], I, 1960, 146-147.

[2] Cf. Asín Palacios *Logia et agrapha*, 423-424.

[3] Cf. Najm *Das biographische Lexikon*, 405-406.

[4] Tottoli *Jesus and the skull*, 230-231.

[5] Cf. Farīd ad-Dīn 'Aṭṭār *Elāhī-nāme*, 352-353; Bernardini *Peregrinazioni letterarie*. The man brought back to life by Jesus is called *Ḥayyān bin Ma'bad*.

[6] Cf. Pennacchietti *Il racconto di Giomgiomé*.

[7] Cf. Pennacchietti *Teschio redivivo*, 113-114.

subject, *Qaṣīdat al-jumjuma* ('the skull poem'), is clearly of different origin.[1] In order to have an idea of the extent of the success of the legend of *Jesus and the skull* in Sufi circles, especially in Khorasan and Central Asia, it is enough to remember four lines of a work by the great Persian poet and mystic Jalāl ad-Dīn Rūmī (1207-1273), who was, like Isḥāq bin Bishr, a native of Balkh:

> If you should see a cut-off skull
> That rolling comes upon My plain,
> Beware, ask it about the Arcana.
> From it you'll learn My hidden secret![2]

The spread of the legend of *Jesus and the skull* prompted a certain devotion among the masses to the figure of the king who became an ascetic. Indeed, widely scatterd localities lay claim to the site of his venerated tomb.[3]

However, the legend of *Jesus and the skull* is also widespread among Eastern Christians,[4] where the character of the 'skull king' curiously takes the name of 'Abbot Arsenius king of Egypt'. This may be a folk reflection of the figure of St. Arsenius

---

[1] Cf. Pennacchietti *Gesù e Bālwān*. In the poem in Maghribi Arabic the man Jesus restores to life is called *Bālwān bin Ḥafṣ bin Daylam* in accordance with the Hispano-Arabic model of Abū Bakr aṭ-Ṭarṭūshī

[2] In Persian: *čo dar rah bebini boride sar i / ke ghalṭān ravad suy e meidān e mā // az u pors az u pors asrār e mā / k az u beshnavi serr e penhān e mā*, cf. Moulānā Jalāl ad-Dīn Rūmī, *Kollīyāt-e shams yā Dīvān-e kabīr*, ed. Badī' az-Zamān Furūzānfarr, Tehran 2535, I, 150. I am grateful to Anna Krasnowolska of the University of Krakow for indicating these lines to me.

[3] As regards the veneration of the tomb of the 'king Skull' (*Jomjome Solṭān*) in Anatolia, see Cunbur *Cimcime Sultan*. A photograph of his sepulchre at Derbent in Daghestan, the *Portae Caspiae* of the ancients, may be found as Tab. VIIIa in Cuneo *Le mura*. Another tomb of 'king Skull', a site of pilgrimage, is in Nedroma, in western Algeria, near Tlemcen, cf. "Nédroma" in *E.I.*[1], II, 1936, 968-969; and Massignon *Parole donnée*, 380. Here the 'king Skull' is called *Sīdī Solṭān* 'my Lord Sultan' or *Ra's bin Ādam* 'Head (of the?) son of Adam'. A further tomb of 'king Skull' was seen on 29.11.1616 by Pietro della Valle near Hilla in the south-western corner of the ruins of Babylon in Iraq. Cf. Pennacchietti *Osservazioni*, 266.

[4] Regarding the Christian compositions in verse and prose on the "king Skull", see Pennacchietti *Versione neoaramaica*, and idem *Teschio redivivo* . Such compositions have been found in the Arabic, Syriac, North-Eastern Neo-Aramaic and Georgian languages.

the Great (c. 353-450), an anchorite of the Egyptian desert and Father of the Church. All the same, I do not think it is a case of late hagiographic contamination, because the legend of *Jesus and the skull* may have taken form in pre-Islamic times, thanks to the coalescence of hagiographic elements regarding various saints, first among whom was St. George. Among the sensational miracles attributed to this much-loved saint, he is said to have restored to life the bones of an idolator named Yubal, who had been condemned to Hell.[1] The possibility cannot, then, be ruled out that in the course of the centuries two parallel versions of the legend of *Jesus and the skull* may have co-existed: one Christian, the other Islamised.

5.3.2 *The narrative structure of the Story of the skull and the king*

A simple comparison of the *Story of the skull and the king* with one of the many prose or verse editions of the legend of *Jesus and the skull* demonstrates that the two tales are very closely related. Not only do they both deal with an eschatological topic, but they also share two fundamental moments: 1) the discovery of a human skull as the starting point for reflections on the afterlife; 2) the motif of the 'hero who becomes a hermit'. Closer examination brings to light singular coincidences which can only be explained on the hypothesis that the *Story of the skull and the king* depends on the legend of *Jesus and the skull.*

As regards the motif of the discovery of a skull, it is certainly no mere chance that both the Israelite king and Jesus react in the same way when confronted by this miserable sample of mortal remains: both wonder whose it can be. Compare the following passages.

Story of the skull and the king

(fol. 32c) While he was wandering disconsolately in the cave he saw an enormous, decayed skull, than which he had never seen anything more terrifying. Turning it over and over, he was astonished at its size, and said: (fol. 32b)...'If only I knew who this

[1] Cf. Pennacchietti *San Giorgio*, 101-104; idem *Il racconto di Giomgiomé*, 105-106.

skull had belonged to! To a king or an aristocrat, a wretch or a respectable man, a poor man or a rich?'

Jesus and the skull, Persian edition of 'Aṭṭār:
Then Jesus went towards that head,
Saying to it: 'O skull! For God's sake
Come, tell me your whole story!
Were you once plain or were you handsome?
Were you from Heaven or from Hell?
Did you act in a miserly or a generous fashion?
Did you have power or were you a subject?
Were you a poor man or even a king?'[1]

In the Arabic edition of *Jesus and the skull* in Maghribi verse, the questions about the dead man's identity occupy no fewer than 24 of the 128 stanzas, one-fifth of the poem, and review all the possible roles, professions and trades that the skull's owner may have fulfilled during his life.[2]

In the *Story of the skull and the king*, the questions obviously remain unanswered, but still serve to prompt the meditation on human destiny after death. In contrast, in *Jesus and the skull* the same questions immediately trigger a conversation between the prophet and the skull, which miraculously regains the power of speech.

Turning to the coincidence regarding the motif of the 'hero who becomes a hermit', it is illustrated by the following extracts:

Story of the skull and the king:
(fol. 44b) '... after yielding the kingdom to his son, he went up to the cloister where Susanna had lived. There he worshipped God – He is mighty and exalted – with great fervour until his last hour came, and when he died, God had mercy on him.'

Jesus and the skull, Persian version of 'Aṭṭār:
The new Jomjome was drawn to faith.
He was converted and chose the religion of Christ.
He became a believer with some difficulty
But then lived with faith and true religion.
With continual fasting he did penance,

---

[1] Cf. Pennacchietti *Il racconto di Giomgiomé*, 96, vv. 15-18.

[2] Cf. Pennacchietti *Gesù e Bālwān*, 152-156, strophes 19-43.

only every forty days he took food.[1]

Maghribi Arabic version:
He made a solemn profession of faith and went off praising God.
For seventy years he lived as a hermit until he died a good Muslim.[2]

Neo-Aramaic Christian version:
When Christ raised me, he took me to himself and baptised me, and made me live on the mountain of the ascetics.[3]

It is, then, highly likely that the unknown author of the *Story of the skull and the king* was inspired by *Jesus and the skull.* His model must have been an ancient Arabic edition of this legend. We have seen that in the time of the traditionalist Isḥāq bin Bishr (d. 821) it was already known over a wide area, as far afield as Bukhara. The author of the novella may be supposed to have used the themes of the discovery of a skull and the decision to withdraw to a hermitage as the two pillars to support the daring structure of his tale. In this sense, *Jesus and the skull* is to be considered the foundation of the whole narrative structure of the *Story of the skull and the king.*

6 The dating problem

Apart from the fact that it is anonymous, the *Story of the skull and the king* offers no external clue which would help to determine its date of composition. The miscellaneous Arabic manuscript which contains it (Gotha orient. A 2756) is also undated, though relatively recent. This is why the only trustworthy criteria for chronological evaluation are text-internal, i.e. it is necessary to identify in the script those orthographic, morphological and lexical characteristics which are recognised as peculiar to a particular phase in the evolution of the Arabic language. Now, a comparison of the data supplied by our text with those noted by Simon Hopkins in Arabic papyruses prior to 912 AD reveals a

---

1 Cf. Pennacchietti *Il racconto di Giomgiomé*, 99, vv. 74-76.

2 Cf. Pennacchietti *Gesù e Bālwān*, 168-169, strophe 122.

3 Cf. Pennacchietti *Teschio redivivo*, 115, strophe 35.

very high percentage of orthographic and linguistic coincidences between the *Story of the skull and the king* and the Arab texts from that period.[1]

Another element which may be decisive for the chronological definition of the novella is its title: *Ḥadīth al-jumjuma ma'a l-malik*. The term *ḥadīth* slowly changed into a specifically religious technical term with the specific meaning of documented tradition regarding the sayings or doings of the Prophet. The presence of *ḥadīth* in the title may therefore indicate – as is true of the *Ḥadīth Dāwud*, the *Story of David* attributed to Wahb bin Munabbih (§ 2.3) – that the *Story of the skull and the king* was fixed in written form in a period when this word was still used without difficulty for any type of story. From Khoury[2] we learn that after the middle of the 9th century the situation underwent a radical change. From that time, even stories of the biblical prophets were designated with the profane term *qiṣṣa*, pl. *qiṣaṣ*, 'story, tale, narration'. It remains to be seen whether the other texts in MS orient. A 2756 in Gotha with the word *ḥadīth* 'story, tale'[3] in their titles, namely *Ḥadīth Ṣāliḥ wa-n-nāqa*, a story about the prophet Ṣāliḥ and his female camel, and *Ḥadīth 'Abdillāh bin al-Mubāraka ma'a Rābi'a al-'Adawīya*, a story about the Sufi 'Abdullāh bin al-Mubâraka (d. 796) and the mystic Rābi'a al-'Adawīya (d. 801), confirm so early a date.

The orthography and language of our novella, and above all the use of the word *ḥadīth* in the title lead us, therefore, to put it in the period before the middle of the 9th century. It should be noted that this chronological collocation, though admittedly approximate, corresponds to a period in which Islamic culture – which had recently found its definitive identity – was still powerfully receptive of and malleable by the cultural and religious traditions of most of the population of the new empire: the Christian, Jewish, Samaritan and Zoroastrian subjects, and those affiliated to the various gnostic and synchretistic sects.

The clear relationship of dependence of the Arabian episode of Susanna on the Samaritan variant of the biblical tale (§ 4.3.1)

---

[1] Cf. Hopkins *Early Arabic*.

[2] Cf. Khoury *Kalif, Geschichte und Dichtung*, 208-209; idem *Mille et Une Nuits*, 31-33.

[3] Thanks to Pertsch's catalogue (*Gotha*, IV, 464) and to an *excipit* marked on folio 30a, I was able to identify two of them.

may indicate that Damascus in the Umayyad period or at the beginning of the Abbasid period was where the *Story of the skull and the king* was composed. These must be the time and place in which the first and perhaps the only fertile encounter between Islam and Samaritan culture took place, in a cosmopolitan city where the Samaritans had a community which was still flourishing and prestigious.

7 Conclusion

The *Story of the skull and the king* is an admonitory novella on an eschatological theme which belongs, like the legend of *Jesus and the skull* (§ 5.3.1), to the ancient literary genre of the *Isrā'īlīyāt*, pious tales on the *Banū Isrā'īl*, as the first centuries of Islam designated the monotheists of the preceding period. Indeed, the protagonist of the tale, the unnamed king who is Susanna's grandfather, is expressly defined as 'Israelite', and obviously Susanna and the son of Zechariah are Israelites.

The novella seems to have been composed by a *qāṣṣ*, a popular narrator and preacher, who probably lived not later than the middle of the 9th century, and was well versed in Jewish, Samaritan and Christian traditions, with which his profession would have constrained him to be familiar. At the same time the anonymous author is moved by a profound ascetic and mystic tension. The *Story of the skull and the king* was, in fact, inspired by one of the loftiest themes in Islamic spirituality: the ennobling and sanctifying power of suffering. This theme is developed in three different chapters, each of which corresponds to one stage on the Sufi path of spiritual ascesis.

The first chapter (§ 4: fol. 30a-32a), by way of preamble, describes how the still uncertain, immature faith of a pre-Islamic king is tested.

In chapter 2 (fol. 32a-36b) the subjects dealt with are unbelief and suffering, an element necessary to redemption.

Chapter 3 (fol. 36b-44a) provides an account of the various phases of the hero's repentance, culminating in the epilogue (fol. 44b) with the expiation of his sin of incredulity by means of abdication and withdrawal to ascetic life.

The Arab novella is at the centre of a close-knit network of narrative traditions. On the one hand, it offers a further variation on the narrative theme of *Susanna*, a biblical tale which seems to go back to an Indo-European archetype (§ 1.2.3); at the same time, it is the first example of reworking of the widespread Islamic legend of *Jesus and the skull*, which gave rise in Central Asia to interesting developments. The pattern of this ancient legend provided the author of the novella with the basis for a composite but original plot, arranged in three strata which correspond to the three chapters mentioned above.

The first of these strata is dominated by the Old-Oriental motif of the 'hunter king' and the archetype of the 'animal guide' or the 'hunted cervid' who leads the hero into a wonderful adventure (§ 4.1). Parallels with medieval European literature readily spring to mind, from both religious and profane contexts. Narrative themes of this kind are frequent in Christian hagiography, and also in the Breton romances of the 12th and 13th centuries. Many 'hunter heroes' who were to become saints are said to have met a marvellous deer in the forest, from St. Eustace to St. Giles, from St. Hubert of Lièges to St. Julian the Hospitaller and St. Meinulf.

The second stratum of the plot contains a no less important archetypal motif: the 'Tree of Youth' or 'Tree of Life' (§ 4.2). The origin of this motif can be traced to the Christian legend of the *Wood of the Cross*, whose roots are in apocryphal Jewish texts.

The third and last stratum is represented by a remarkable reworking of the tale of 'Susanna and the elders' (*Daniel* 13). This episode, which has inspired many painters of the stature of Pinturicchio, Tintoretto, Veronese, Tiepolo, Rubens and Rembrandt, as well as composers such as Händel and Hindemith, is radically transformed (§ 4.3). In place of a beautiful young woman, surprised by indiscreet watchers in the privacy of her garden, we have a young princess, vulnerable but full of energy and drive, who lives in a hermitage in the desert.

It may be that the echo of this reworking reached the ears of Giovanni Boccaccio. As is well known, Boccaccio spent many years in Neaples, which was one of the most important trading centres in the Mediterranean, in close contact with the Muslim world. Boccaccio may have been inspired by the *Story of the skull and the king* or simply by the episode of Susanna when he composed what amounts to a parody, the *Tale of Alibech and Rustico* (*Decameron* III, 10), a novella whose antecedent has not yet been identified.

It would also seem that the *Story of the skull and the king*, without the episode of Susanna, survived – though in radically different form – in a strange religious legend of medieval France, the 13th-century *Romanz de Saint Fanuel et de Sainte Anne* (§ 4.2). By what route and in what period can it have reached French folklore? Very likely by way of Muslim Spain. It must be recollected that the legend of *Jesus and the skull*, to which our novella owes something, was known between the 11th and 12th centuries to the Arab-Catalan man of letters Abū Bakr aṭ-Ṭarṭūshī.

It is surprising that the *Story of the skull and the king*, echoes of which seem to have reached medieval France and Italy, should have been forgotten in Arab literature. We have no news of it but through a solitary manuscript, a miscellaneous Arab codex from Gotha which includes edifying tales, stories of mystics and prayers. We may hope to trace it in other manuscripts of the same kind, i.e. in texts linked to the activity of the *quṣṣāṣ*, the earliest Islamic preachers. This literary production is, however, of a popular, self-contradictory nature, and of marginal importance. From the beginning of the 14th century it had been continually rejected by official Arabic culture. In the imaginative tales of the pre-Islamic patriarchs and prophets (the *Isrā'īlīyāt*), medieval authors of the stature of Ibn Taymiyya (d. 1328) and Ibn Kathīr (d. 1372-3), down to authoritative modern thinkers such as Muḥammad 'Abduh (d. 1905), have seen only extravagant subjects, spread surreptitiously by Hebrew and Christian converts, the fruit of their ignorance, if not their lies.[1]

Even such edifying tales as the *Story of the skull and the king* have been the object of disapproval and rejection. Though pervaded by Sufi spirituality and unconcerned with doctrinal matters, they have been accused of drawing freely on the pre-Islamic cultural heritage.

The publication of this ancient novella is an attempt to recover certain factors of continuity which, at least in terms of narrative, have for centuries linked the new civilisation inaugurated by Islam with its undeniable roots in late antiquity.

---

[1] Cf. Tottoli *Il rifiuto*.

THE QUEEN OF SHEBA, THE GLASS FLOOR AND THE FLOATING TREE-TRUNK[1]

1. The Queen of Sheba in the Scriptures

The Queen of Sheba, together with Eve, Sarah, Hagar, Rebecca and Susanna, is one of the very limited number of female Old Testament characters who appear not only in Jewish but also in Christian-inspired and, finally, Islamic literature. This privileged position derives from the fact that she is named in the sacred writings of all three of the revealed religions. What varies considerably, however, from one sacred text to another is the tone in which her meeting with Solomon is recounted.[2]

The pericopes dealing with the Queen of Sheba in the Old[3]

---

[1] The Italian original version has been presented to the journal "Sincronie", published by the University of Rome "Tor Vergata", Dipartimento di Studi Filologici, Linguistici e Letterari (IV,7 [2000], 48-64). The English text has been revised and updated with respect to the Italian original.

[2] A documentary by Martin Messonnier, entitled 'Sur les traces de la reine de Saba. À la recherche d'une figure de légende au Yémen, en Israël et en Éthiopie', was shown on the evening of Sunday 7 November 1999 on the Franco-German television channel Arte. It was preceded by King Vidor's film 'Solomon and the Queen of Sheba', starring Yul Brynner and Gina Lollobrigida.

[3] Cf. *1 Kings* 10:1-10,13: '(1) The queen of Sheba heard of Solomon's fame and came to test him with difficult questions. (2) She arrived in Jerusalem with a very large retinue, with camels laden with spices and an immense quantity of gold and precious stones. Having reached Solomon, she discussed with him everything that she had in mind, (3) and Solomon had an answer for all her questions; not one of them was too obscure for the king to answer for her... (10) And she presented the king with a hundred and twenty talents of gold and great quantities of spices and precious stones; no such wealth of spices ever came again as those which the queen of Sheba gave to King Solomon... (13) And King Solomon, in his turn, presented the queen of Sheba with everything that

and New Testaments[1] are informed by the most irenical universalism. In the first Book of Kings and in Chronicles she is described as an intelligent, wise, generous woman, with not the least hint at the fact that she belonged to a nation of idolatrous Gentiles. Indeed, in the Gospels the tale of the Queen of Sheba who 'came from the ends of the earth to listen to the wisdom of Solomon' is offered as proof of God's predilection for those pagans who have abandoned idol-worship. Together with the Ninivites whom Jonah converted, the 'Queen of the South', as she is called, at the end of time will judge and condemn the generation of Jesus for failing to accept a message of salvation of far greater importance than Solomon's.

In contrast, in the Koran (xxvii, 16-44)[2] the tale of the Queen of Sheba is presented within a framework of fable as an example of the vain erudition of the polytheists. Despite her wit and learning, she cannot hold out against the 'true Knowledge' (v. 42) which God grants to his faithful. The whole passage, in the Koran, is thus pervaded by a spirit of revenge and condemnation of the presumptuousness and arrogance of the idolaters. The Queen of Sheba, however, is converted.

---

she expressed a wish for, besides those presents which he gave her with a munificence worthy of King Solomon. After which, she went home to her own country, she and her servants' (*The New Jerusalem Bible*, London 1985). See also the parallel text in *2 Chronicles* 9:1-9,12.

[1] Cf. *Matthew* 12:42: 'On Judgment Day the Queen of the South will appear against this generation and be its condemnation, because she came from the ends of the earth to hear the wisdom of Solomon; and look, there is something greater than Solomon here' (*The New Jerusalem Bible*, London 1985). See also the parallel text in *Luke* 11:31. The Queen of Sheba is called 'Queen of the South' as in the *Testament of Solomon*, cf. McCown *Testament*: 64*, xxi, 1: ἡ βασίλισσα Νότου.

[2] Cf. *Koran* xxvii 'The *sūra* of the Ant': '(42) So, when [the Queen] came, it was said unto her: "Is thy throne like this?" She answered: "It is as though it were the very one." And Solomon said: "We were given the knowledge before her, and we had surrendered to Allah." (43) And all that she was wont to worship instead of Allah hindered her, for she came of disbelieving folk. (44) It was said unto her: "Enter the hall." And when she saw it she deemed it a pool and bared her legs. Solomon said: "Lo! it is a hall, made smooth of glass." She said: "My Lord! Lo! I have wronged myself, and I surrender with Solomon to Allah, the Lord of the Worlds."' (*The Meaning of the Glorious Koran*, by Mohammed Marmaduke Pickthall, New York, undated; cf. Bausani *Corano*: 275-277).

A further difference to be noted in the accounts given of the Queen of Sheba in the sacred texts of the three religions is the way each presents the protagonist. In the Old Testament and in the Koran she is a proud woman of outstanding intelligence; but whereas, in the Jewish text, it is she who puts Solomon's wisdom to the test with her abstruse riddles, in the Koran it is Solomon who uses two marvels to test the Queen's powers of judgment.

There is nothing of this in the Gospels, where the Queen of Sheba is a deeply religious woman, thirsty for knowledge and ready to confront any difficulty in the pursuit of her ideal of perfection. No least indication is given of her supposed love of riddles or occult sciences.

These are the premises from which we may begin our examination of how, with notable divergences, repeated points of contact and surprising additions, the narrative threads may be disentangled in the various accounts, in Jewish, Christian and Islamic literatures, of the meeting of the Queen of Sheba with Solomon.

2. Under the sign of the hoopoe

Strange as it may seem, apart from the Old Testament and Gospel data already mentioned, the legend of the Queen of Sheba does not appear in Jewish and Christian contexts until the 10th century, at the height of the Middle Ages. It would appear that for almost a thousand years the official literatures of Judaism and Christianity remained firmly and obstinately silent in the face of popular traditions surrounding the meeting of Solomon with this queen.

It is, however, reasonable to suppose that stories and legends about the power and wisdom of King David's successor were already circulating in Palestine in the first millennium BC, together with tales of the Queen of Sheba's riddles and the supposed marriage of these two extraordinary sovereigns. There were probably details in some of these legends which in later ages, when religious sensibilities had changed, might conflict with the well-established image of Solomon as the highest representation of human wisdom.[1] The fact remains that there is no mention of

---

[1] Cf. *1 Kings* 5:9-14: '(9) God gave Solomon immense wisdom and understanding, and a heart as vast as the sand on the sea-shore. (10) The wisdom of Solomon surpassed the wisdom of all the sons of the East and

his relationship with the Queen of Sheba in the Jerusalem Talmud, nor in the Babylonian Talmud, nor in the oldest *Midrashim*,[1] nor in any other kind of rabbinical literature.

Christian literature, despite its greater breadth and detail, is in this respect no different from Jewish sources. There was an unwritten law forbidding public treatment of a subject which was regarded as taboo. It is, however, worth recollecting that the first mention of the Queen of Sheba in mediaeval Latin literature goes back to the middle of the 9th century. John of Seville, in a letter to Álvaro Paulo (d. 861), a prominent representative of the church in the Caliphate of Cordova, explains to him that Mohammed, the prophet of Islam, composed 'psalms' in which animals appeared. The protagonists of one of these 'psalms' are the frog (*rana*) and the hoopoe. *Rana* is clearly an erroneous copying of *reina*, 'queen'.[2]

In these circumstances, there is obviously great value in the evidence of those verses of the Koran which relate to the Queen of Sheba, and in the comments and sermons of early Islam which touch on this subject. Furthermore, the oldest Islamic tradition offers confirmation of the quality and great antiquity of those versions of the legend passed down in mediaeval Jewish manuscripts.

It is a legend which must already have been firmly rooted in the collective imagination of the Arab peoples in the time of the Prophet Mohammed. Many settlers in the Arabian peninsula, especially in Yemen, were Israelites, and in the northern fringes of the desert, in Syria and Mesopotamia, various nomadic tribes had embraced Christianity. Hence the Koran text has no need to expatiate on details, but simply describes the essence of the situation with flashes of allusion, bringing it to life in the hearers' minds. Far more space is dedicated, in the same passage, to eulogies and declarations of submission to the One God. From Jewish tradition and from the first commentaries on the Koran, the plot may be

---

all the wisdom of Egypt. (11) He was wiser than anyone else... (13) He could discourse on plants from the cedar in Lebanon to the hyssop growing on the wall; and he could discourse on animals and birds and reptiles and fish. (14) Men from all nations came to hear Solomon's wisdom, and he received gifts from all the kings in the world.'

[1] Homiletic commentaries on the Scriptures.

[2] Cf. D'Alverny *La connaissance*, 588-599.

reconstructed as follows:

> Solomon, who loved banquets and feasts, presented an extraordinary spectacle one day to the kings of the Orient: a parade of devils, spirits and animals from heaven and earth. The only creature missing was the hoopoe, which arrived late, explaining by way of excuse that it had just discovered, at the end of the earth, a very wealthy country governed by a woman. The bird promised to bring her to Solomon's feet in chains, if the king wished.
>
> Solomon was delighted and gave the hoopoe a letter ordering the queen to come and pay him homage; otherwise the birds, the spirits and the demons would conquer her country at his command. In reply the queen sent a letter and costly gifts, and set out at once on the journey.
>
> When after seven years' travelling she reached Jerusalem, Solomon welcomed her at the royal baths (according to Jewish sources) or in a pavilion with a glass floor (according to the Koran). This unusual welcome disconcerted the queen, who mistook the floor of the foyer for an expanse of water. So, as she crossed the threshold, she raised the hem of her dress just enough to prevent it from getting wet.[1]
>
> This momentary confusion on the part of the queen allowed Solomon to admire her legs, but also to realise that they were much too hairy. Disappointed, he provoked her with a far from courteous remark: 'Madam, your beauty is feminine, but the hair on your legs is masculine. Well, hairy legs are fine for a man but revolting on a woman'.[2] The queen's pride was hurt, and she reacted by putting a long series of riddles to Solomon, only to discover, to her astonishment, that he was cleverer than she, for he solved them without difficulty. And so she praised and worshipped the One God, and after receiving all she most desired from Solomon she took her leave.

This, in short, is the plot of the story in the *Targūm Shenī*, a collection of homilies, in Aramaic, on the book of Esther, which is thought to have been composed at the end of the 7th or the beginning of the 8th century, though it is unrecorded until the 11th century.

---

[1] On the gesture of raising the hem of a garment when crossing a stretch of water, see Isaiah 47:2.

[2] Cf. Grossfeld *Targum Sheni*, 115-116.

What distinguishes this version from every other, Jewish or Islamic, is a detail which would confirm its antiquity. In the Jewish version, Solomon receives the Queen in his private baths, whereas in the Islamic version they are in a glass building[1] or in a palace with a glass floor.[2] The difference is not without significance, though the result is identical: irrespective of the exact setting, the Queen in any case mistakenly believes that she is standing before a stretch of water. I believe, however, that it is more likely that the shiny floor of a bath is transformed into the glass or crystal paving of an enchanted palace, rather than vice versa.

3. The Jewish and Islamic versions: an aetiological account

All the versions, whether Jewish or Islamic, share a dominant characteristic in the transposition of the figure of Solomon from the dimension of myth attributed to him in the Bible[3] to that of the wonderful and esoteric.[4] This is why the slight figure of the hoopoe[5] appears in the tale with remarkable duties. This bird, whose delicacy is counterbalanced by the brilliance of its tall erectile tuft, symbolises that subtle universe where anything is

---

[1] Cf. Ginzberg *Legends*, IV, 145.

[2] *Koran* xxvii, 44. The Solomonic theme of the glass floor is found in the *lambda* edition of the *Romance of Alexander* (early 8th century), cf. Trumpf *Alexander*. In this Byzantine text Alexander describes to his mother Olympia how he was welcomed in the palace of Candace, Queen of Ethiopia. He too believed at first that he was going into a covered pool.

[3] Cf. *1 Kings* 5:9-14; *Matthew* 6:28-29; *Luke* 12:27.

[4] Solomon is supposed to have received from the archangel Michael a magic ring which gave him power over devils, cf. Schürer *Storia*, 490-495; *Koran* xxxviii, 36-38: '(36) So We made subservient to him... - (37) the devils, every builder and diver, - (38) and others linked together in chains' (*The Meaning of the Glorious Koran*, New York, undated).

[5] The hoopoe, whose name imitates the call ('po-po-po') it gives during the mating season, is in Hebrew called *dūkīfat*, in Jewish and Syriac Aramaic *tarnāgol barrā* (literally 'wild cockerel'), in Arabic *hudhud*, in North-Eastern Neo-Aramaic *hāpūpkā*, *hudhud* and also *ṭērā d-malkā Šlēmūn*, 'King Solomon's bird', and in Kurdish *pepūsil, manke*, 'Solomon's owl'.

possible.[1] It is a member of the numberless hosts of creatures of heaven and earth, of demons and spirits, which obey the orders of the King, build him magnificent palaces and travel to the ends of the earth to bring him whatever he wants. Solomon knows their language and has a sovereign familiarity with them. And in any case, the hoopoe has always been regarded as creature of peculiar authority: this is the bird which, in Aristophanes, guards the heavenly gates of the 'City of the Birds',[2] and which leads the other birds to their mystical encounter with the Phoenix.[3]

Balancing the exaltation of the supernatural powers granted by God to the King of Judah, the figure of the Queen of Sheba has been somewhat demonised[4] and in the best cases presented ambiguously. Medieval Jewish tradition considers her neither more nor less than a witch,[5] while for the commentators of the Koran, she is a hybrid creature, part human and part jinn.[6] This is why they see her as distinguished by certain carefully hidden androgynous features, such as excessively hairy legs.

On this subject the Koranic exegetes have taken up the rumour which relates that the demons who were subjugated by Solomon made him believe that, under her clothes, the Queen was

---

[1] Cf. Bausani *Corano*, 612; Venzlaff *Al-Hudhud*, 83-121. The hoopoe is in a sense an ambiguous creature: apart from its call, which is often mistaken for the hooting of an owl or the barking of a dog, it is also known to the classical Arab writers by its repulsive smell, cf. Venzlaff *Al-Hudhud*: 64-67; 113-117. This may be why the Torah (*Leviticus* 11:19) counts it among the impure animals which may not be eaten.

[2] It is probable that in popular Greek etymology ἔποψ 'hoopoe' was connected with ἐπόπτης 'supervisor, inspector', cf. Ribezzo *Ibrido*: 108. Ἐπόπτης, in the sense 'contemplator', also designated the initiate to the highest level of the Eleusinian mysteries.

[3] This is the subject of the wisdom poem *Manṭiq aṭ-ṭayr* 'The logic of the birds' by the Persian mystic Farīd ad-Dīn 'Aṭṭār (1119-1220?), see Carlo Saccone *Il verbo*.

[4] Cf. Lassner *Demonizing the Queen of Sheba*.

[5] Cf. Ginzberg *Legends*, IV, 152; Duling *Testament*, 983, ch. xxi, 1-4.

[6] She was said to be the daughter of a human prince and of a princess of the jinns, cf. Grünbaum *Sagenkunde*, 219; Canova *Bilqìs*, 25-27; 64. The Arabic term *jinn* designates a specific kind of spirits: fire genies (*Koran* xv, 27), invisible creatures who are sometimes friendly, sometimes hostile towards humans.

concealing the hooves of a donkey.[1] This being so, it is understandable that the king should have prepared one of his most brilliant tricks to check the veracity of this suggestion: the illusion of the stretch of water in his baths or in the crystal floor of his palace.

The sequel to this story may be of interest. When he discovered the truth, Solomon was angry with the demons for lying to him, and by way of reparation ordered them to invent a depilatory that should be as drastic as it was effective. They duly produced a compound of arsenic and quicklime,[2] and thanks to their ointment the Queen of Sheba's attractiveness became proverbial.[3] The Prophet Mohammed is supposed to have said that the queen was 'one of the women with the most gorgeous legs' and that she was 'among the brides of Solomon in Paradise'. This enthusiasm on the Prophet's part did not please his young wife, Aisha, in the least, and she insisted on knowing whether the queen's legs were better than her own. Her prudent husband willingly acknowledged that his wife's legs were even more gorgeous.[4]

3.1 *Two discourteous epithets*

3.1.1 '*The hairy woman*'

The whole narrative structure of the Jewish and Islamic versions turns, in effect, on the trick Solomon arranges to establish whether the queen is a human being or a devil. It is as though the only really important aspect of the meeting of the two sovereigns in Jerusalem were the rumours of the queen's excessively hairy legs.

In the Near East, as in the rest of the world, there is a rooted

---

[1] Cf. Hertz *Die Rätsel*, 10; Grünbaum *Sagenkunde*, 219; Canova *Bilqìs*, 34, 85.

[2] Cf. Ginzberg *Legends*, VI, 289, note 41; Canova *Bilqìs*, 36, 91.

[3] Cf. Herr *La Reine*, 9. According to an *exemplum* written in the 13th century by a French Dominican, the Queen of Sheba was moved by her unhappy experience with the mirrored floor of the royal hall (*pavimentum aulae regiae plenum speculis*) to set the fashion for long skirts (*adinvenit vestes longas mulieribus*): n° 888 of the *Compilacio singularis exemplorum*, MS C. 523 of the University Library, Uppsala.

[4] Cf. Canova *Bilqìs*, 36.

belief that witches or female devils are hirsute. However, St John (Abdullah) Philby[1] suggests that interest in the supposed hairiness of the Queen of Sheba is due to entirely incidental external interference: confusion of the Queen of Sheba with a famous Arabian queen about whose physical appearance unkind rumours abound. Philby identifies this latter queen with Zenobia, queen of Tadmor, that is, Palmyra.[2]

There are at least three reasons for giving serious consideration to the British scholar's hypothesis, for three points may link the Queen of Sheba and Solomon on the one hand, with this queen of the 3rd century AD on the other.

a) In both the Old Testament and Josephus, the belief is recorded that it was Solomon who built Palmyra;[3] this belief is repeated in later Jewish tradition.[4]

b) Both Jewish and Islamic texts maintain that the Queen of Sheba was buried at Palmyra.[5]

c) Queen Zenobia is known to Arab tradition by the nickname az-Zabbā', 'the hairy woman'.[6]

Now, thanks to the evidence of inscriptions, we know that this is a misunderstanding. Zenobia was never called 'the hairy

---

[1] Cf. Philby *The Queen*, 83-88.

[2] Zenobia, queen of Palmyra (267-272) and *Augusta* of the Roman Empire (171), was the widow of Septimius Odenatus (Uḏaynat) and mother of Vaballathus (Wahballāt), *dux Romanorum* and *imperator*, who shared the throne of Palmyra with her. After her defeat at the hands of Aurelianus, she was taken to Italy. She died at an advanced age near Tivoli, cf. Pauly 1972, 1-8.

[3] Cf. *1 Kings* 9:18 (*tāmār ba-mmidbār* 'Tamar in the desert') and *2 Chronicles* 8:4 (*tadmor ba-mmidbār* 'Palmyra in the desert'), and *Jewish Antiquities* VIII, 2, cf. Niese *Ant. Iud.*, 210, § 154, ll. 9-11. In the massoretic text the place name *tāmār* ('palm') of *1 Kings* 9:18 is read as *tadmor*, which is the original Semitic name of Palmyra.

[4] Cf. Ginzberg *Legends*, IV, 149.

[5] Cf. Ginzberg *Legends*, VI, 291, note 53; Canova *Bilqìs*, 21; her tomb is said to have been discovered in Palmyra during the reign of the Umayyad caliph Walīd I (705-707), cf. Hertz *Die Rätsel*, 10.

[6] Arab tradition is unaware of both the Greek and the Semitic names of Zenobia (later translated as Zaynab). In the Arabic dictionary *Tāj al-'Arūs* ('The bride's crown'), compiled towards the end of the 18th century, there is mention of the hypothetical names Bāri'a, Nābila and Maysūn (Cairo 1306/1889, I, 284).

woman' in Aramaic or in Greek. In the language of Palmyra her name was Bat-Zabbay,[1] and this leads me to believe that, with time, oral tradition changed, to the point of unrecognisability, a name whose meaning was no longer clear. In the Jewish legend in which Zenobia is mentioned, she is called Zamzamay;[2] elsewhere a new etymology has been invented, linking the element Zabbay[3] to the Aramaic and Arabic root *ZBB*, which means 'to be hairy'. Hence the Arab nickname az-Zabbā' 'the hairy woman'.[4]

Once this physical imperfection of the Queen of Palmyra had been transferred to the figure of the Queen of Sheba, the aetiological tale would naturally arise. How did Solomon realise that the Queen of Sheba had hairy legs?

3.1.2 '*The donkey-legged woman*'

Philby's hypothesis that the Queen of Sheba is to be identified with Zenobia can be contested along lines which I believe have not previously been considered.

In his *Jewish Antiquities* Josephus Flavius (38 - c. 102 AD) calls the Queen of Sheba *Nikaule* or *Nikaulis*[5] and identifies her, quoting Herodotus, with an Egyptian queen who lived perhaps at

---

[1] See the bilingual Greek-Aramaic inscriptions *CIS* 3947 and 3971 (Part II, Vol. III, 119-120, 151-153), where the queen is called, in Greek, Σεπτιμία Ζηνοβία ἡ λαμπροτάτη βασίλισσα and in Aramaic SPṬMY' BTZBY NHYRT' MLKT' [*Sepṭemyā Bath-Zabbay nahhīrtā malekthā*], or 'Septimia Zenobia / Bat-Zabbay illustrious queen'. Bat-Zabbay is a personal name meaning 'daughter of Zabbay', *i.e.* descendant of Zabbay, Ζαββαῖος transcribed in Greek, probably the first forefather of the tribe to which the queen belonged; cf. Stark *Personal Names*, 12, 41, 80.

[2] Ginzberg *Legends*, VI, 404, note 45.

[3] The name Zabbay <ZBY> is explained by Stark *Personal Names*, 86 as a hypocorism or abbreviation of a theophoric name written <ZBDBWL> 'gift of Bol'.

[4] Chivalrously, Muḥammad Murtaḍā (1732-1791), author of the *Tāj al-'Arūs*, interprets the term az-Zabbā' as 'long-haired woman', since it is related that when the queen let down her hair, it covered her completely (*op. cit.*, 284).

[5] *Jewish Antiquities* VIII, 2: Νικαύλη or Νίκαυλις cf. Niese *Ant. Iud.*, 211, § 158, l. 13.

the end of the sixth dynasty: Herodotus calls her *Nikotris*.[1] This is why critics unanimously consider the name *Nikaule/Nikaulis* a copying error already present in the manuscript of Herodotus' *Histories* which was consulted by Josephus.[2]

The Greek names *Nikaule* and *Nikaulis*,[3] not recorded elsewhere, might represent a reinterpretation of, respectively, *NQWLH and *NQWLYS. This is how I reconstruct the rendering in Hebrew or Aramaic script of two nicknames which the Greeks habitually gave to Empusa, the female demon famous for having the legs of a donkey:[4] these nicknames were *Onokole* and *Onokolis*,[5] 'the donkey-legged woman'.[6]

What has this terrifyingly ambiguous figure to do with the Queen of Sheba and Solomon? We may well ask – yet the *Testament of Solomon*, a Judaeo-Christian work[7] dated between the 1st and 3rd centuries AD, mentions this very Empusa in connection with our two distinguished personages.[8] The name given her in the *Testament* is not, it is true, either Empusa or *Onokole/Onokolis*, but *Onoskelis*; but this is of very little account, since this nickname too means 'donkey-legged woman'.

The same Judaeo-Christian text tells us that *Onoskelis* (=

---

[1] Νίτωκρις, cf. Herodotus *Histories*, II, 100.

[2] Cf. Hertz *Die Rätsel*, 25.

[3] The names Νικαύλη and Νίκαυλις are compounded respectively from νίκη 'victory' and αὐλή 'courtyard, entrance; residence' and αὖλις 'dwelling; camp': 'home of victory'.

[4] In Greek tradition Empusa is given the epithets Ὀνοκώλη, Ὀνόκωλις, Ὀνοσκελὶς, Ὀνοσκελῆς, Ὀνόσκελος and Ὀνοπόλη, all of which mean '(woman) with donkey legs', cf. Delatte *Anecdota*, 99, 122, 233, 244, 444, 617, and Etienne *Thesaurus*, col. 2025 and 2039.

[5] Ὀνοκώλη and Ὀνόκωλις from ὄνος 'donkey' and κῶλον 'limb, extremity'.

[6] The phenomenon of omission of initial vowel in the transcription of a term of Greek origin (*NQWLH/*NQWLYS for Ὀνοκώλη /Ὀνόκωλις) can be found in Syriac, e.g. *pīṭrōpā,* in Greek ἐπίτροπος 'prefect', *prōselīnōn,* Greek ἀφροσέληνον, 'selenite', *qlēsīs*, Greek ἐκκλησίαι, 'churches', cf. Brockelmann *Lexicon*, 565b, 602a, 669a.

[7] On Judaeo-Christianity see Manns *L'Israel.*

[8] Cf. Duling *Testament*, 964-965, ch. IV. Between 366 and 384 the so-called Ambrosiaster, in his *Comment on the Letter of Titus* (*PL* 17, 503), repudiates the reliability of the *Testament of Solomon,* which is truly an encyclopaedia of demonology.

Onokolis = *Nikaulis*) took an active part in the construction of the Temple in Jerusalem,[1] and that the Queen of Sheba was among the first visitors to the site.[2] We also know that the demon *Onoskelis* had a very close relationship with Solomon. In fact, when the King asked her which angel had the power to 'withhold' her, she answered that it was the King's own guardian angel.[3]

We may understand, then, why the Koranic commentators regard the rumours spread by the demons as essential in the economy of the tale – those rumours which related that the Queen of Sheba was hiding the hooves of a donkey under her clothes. The demons were afraid that Solomon might become infatuated with this woman, whom they saw as a dangerous rival, and that he might end by telling her his hidden secrets. Hence the King's curiosity and the cunning strategem he used to ascertain the true nature of the Queen.

In addition, Islamic tradition has always called the Queen of Sheba *Bilqīs*, a name which both Silvestre de Sacy in 1827 and J. Halévy in 1905[4] linked to Josephus' *Nikaulis*. Now that we can trace this back to *Onokolis*, 'the donkey-legged woman', we are in a position to make a more plausible hypothesis regarding the possible chain of transformations undergone by the nickname in a written form of Arabic which as yet lacked diacritics:

[Onokolis] *NQWLYS [Nikaulis] > *BQWLYS > *BQLYS > BLQYS [Bilqīs]

Thus Arab tradition too may preserve the memory of an ancient overlapping and confusion of the Queen of Sheba, now demonised, with the mythological figure of Empusa.[5]

---

[1] The female devil contributed to the building of the Temple by producing hempen ropes.

[2] Cf. Duling *Testament*, 983, ch. xxi.

[3] In Palestinian amulets of the Roman era Solomon is shown as a knight piercing a supine female devil with a spear, cf. Schürer *Storia*, 491-492. This is the prototype of the iconography of St George. It may be that the female figure in question represents *Onoskelis* or *Onokolis*, cf. Bagatti *Altre medaglie*, 332.

[4] Cf. Stiegner *Die Königin*, 118-119, 123-124; Canova *Bilqìs*, 49, note 52.

[5] In an Islamic context the first portrayals of the Queen of Sheba with devils are Persian, from the Timurid period (1387-1469), cf. Nordio

In the light of this hypothesis the Jewish and Islamic versions of the legend of the Queen of Sheba emerge afresh as an aetiological tale, designed to confirm or invalidate the assimilation of the queen into a female demon with the hooves of a donkey.

It seems, moreover, that the *Testament of Solomon*, with the epithet *Onokolis*, and the witness of Josephus, with the name *Nikaulis*, offer evidence of a much earlier period of formation of the legend. It may have arisen in Palestine as early as the 1st century AD, if not even before, in a popular, largely Hellenised environment.

Consequently, to return to Zenobia, I think it more probable that it was not she, with her supposed hairiness, who inspired our legend, but on the contrary, our legend is likely to have made a substantial contribution to the spread in Near-East folklore of the insulting nickname given by posterity to the Queen of Palmyra.

One more point should be made about the Queen of Sheba's presumed donkey hooves. This motif reappeared unexpectedly in Central Europe in the 12th century, but in a strangely modified form: the Queen is said to have been notable for her *pedes anserinos et oculos lucentes ut stellae* (feet of a goose and eyes that shone like stars).[1] This can easily be explained as scribal error (*asininos* ⇨ *ãserinos*). It is in any case a fact that, in 15th and 16th century engravings in Central European countries, the Queen of Sheba is sometimes shown with the webbed feet of a goose as she crosses the stream that separates her from Solomon.[2] As late as the 18th century, according to Herr, there were in France four statues of the Queen of Sheba with the feet of a goose: the so-called 'reine Pédauque'.[3]

4. The Christian legend: a prophetic tale

In the Christian context two strongly contrasting orientations of the legend are recorded, broadly corresponding, on the one

---

Elementi biblici, 85-86, figs. 4 and 5.

[1] Cf. Hertz *Die Rätsel*, 23-24; Larousse *Grand Dictionnaire Universel du XIXe Siècle*, XII, Paris, undated, 490.

[2] Cf. Herr *La Reine*, 17.

[3] Cf. Herr *La Reine*, 31: in the Priory of Saint-Pourçain (Auvergne) and in the churches of Saint-Bénigne, Dijon; Sainte-Marie, Nesles (Champagne) and Saint-Pierre, Nevers.

hand, to Asiatic and Greek Christianity; on the other to African and Latin Christianity.

4.1 In the Greek-Byzantine area there is no documentation of the legend of the Queen of Sheba until the second half of the 9th century. Its distinguishing characteristic is its identification of the queen with Sabbe or Sambethe,[1] the so-called *Sibylla Hebraea*, who is supposed to have foretold the coming of Jesus Christ.[2] In this context the scriptural motif of the riddles which the queen posed to Solomon is still important,[3] whereas the Jewish and Islamic motif of the host of demons who build the Temple on behalf of the King of Isra'el[4] is entirely set aside. In contrast, the version which is established among Christians in the African zone and subsequently in Latin Christianity omits both the riddles and the devils; it is firmly grafted on to what may be called the pearl of Christian tales, the so-called 'Legend of the wood of the Cross'.[5]

The oldest phase of the African and, later, Latin version of the legend seems to me to be reflected in a Coptic Egyptian tale written in Arabic.[6] Briefly, the story is this:

> When it was planned to build the Temple in Jerusalem, it proved impossible to find tools strong enough to cut the necessary huge blocks of stone out of the rock. So Solomon ordered the capture of a chick of the *rukh*, a fabulous bird of enormous

---

[1] Σάββη / Σαμβήθη, cf. Pauly-Wissowa, cols. 2119-2121, s.v. 'Sambethe'.

[2] She is the first of ten sibyls, also known as the *Sibylla Chaldaea* or *Sibylla Persica*, cf. Suidas, *PG* 117, 1343. As a result of this identification the Byzantines called the Queen of Sheba by the name of Sibyl, cf. Nestle *Zur Königin von Saba*, 492-493.

[3] Cf. Hertz *Die Rätsel*, 18-19.

[4] The curious, unforeseen statement of *1 Kings* 6:7, according to which the building of the Temple was to be carried out in complete silence and without using metal tools, evidently fired the imagination of generations of believers, giving rise to fancies from biblical times on. On the other hand, according to one of the precepts of the 'Law of the Covenant' (*Exodus* 20:25), the altar, and by extension the Temple, could not be built of stone hewn with a metal blade. This is why Solomon, according to a widespread old legend, turned for help to the demons, the only intelligent beings, after the angels, capable of building without making use of metal tools.

[5] Cf. Mussafia *Sulla leggenda*; Meyer *Geschichte*; Graf *Leggenda*.

[6] Cf. Bezold *Kebra Nagast*, xlii-lx.

size. The vast chick was promptly caught and put under an upturned copper cauldron in the courtyard of the royal palace. The mother *rukh*, flying over Jerusalem, quickly identified her baby's prison and, determined to set him free, took charge of a huge tree trunk which seemed to have been rolled into position at the bottom of the Garden of Eden for her especial benefit. Making an immense effort, she flew with it over the city and dropped it on to the cauldron, which split in two, releasing the chick unharmed. At this point Solomon ordered the stonebreakers to use this mysterious tree trunk to break the rock and hew the stones. From that moment on, they had no further difficulty. It was sufficient simply to touch the rocky mass with the trunk and it obligingly fell into squares of the required size.[1]

Meanwhile Solomon had been told that the Queen of Sheba, whose imminent arrival in the city had been announced, had one monstrous leg like the hoof of a goat. This was why she had decided to remain a spinster. So the king had the whole esplanade of the Temple flooded, and after putting his throne in a dry spot he waited for the queen to dismount and walk barefoot across the sacred esplanade. Thus the queen was unable to conceal her goatish leg but, as she was wading through the water, she was touched by the mysterious tree trunk, which had floated up to the surface. This touch produced a miracle: the goat's hoof was turned into a human leg, as lovely as the other. When the esplanade was drained, the miraculous trunk was placed in the Temple and the queen adorned it with a silver armlet. With the passing of time, a further 29 silver armlets were laid at the foot of the holy trunk. Later, at the time of the Passion of Jesus, they were all fused together to produce the thirty pieces of silver paid to Judas for his betrayal, while out of the trunk itself was carved the Cross of Christ.

4.2 I believe that this Christian version from Egypt is the foundation for the well-known Ethiopian variant of the legend of the Queen of Sheba,[2] which forms the nucleus and the opening of the 'Glory of the Kings' (*Kebra Nagast*), an early-14th-century

---

[1] By introducing into the tale the motif of the heavenly tree brought by the *rukh*, the Coptic narrator brilliantly did away with the embarrassing presence of the stone-breaking demon builders.

[2] Bezold (*Kebra Nagast*, xlii and lx) holds exactly the opposite opinion, maintaining that the Egyptian tale is directly dependent on the Ethiopian version of the same legend.

work which the Ethiopians still regard as fundamental, the cornerstone of their national identity. Here the tale has been stripped of all that is wonderful and fantastic, even to the riddles. For example, the function – originally the hoopoe's – of describing the glories of the King of Jerusalem to the queen is now fulfilled by a merchant named Tamrin, which serves to give the tale an appearance of historical validity; and this is important, since it is offered as an account of the origin of the Ethiopian dynasty of the Solomonids, a dynasty which was to end, as we know, with the comparatively recent death of the Emperor Haile Selassie.

Of course, the favourite theme is the seduction of the Queen of Sheba by Solomon. On her journey home she is delivered of a child named David, destined to be the founder of the Solomonid dynasty. When he grows up he goes back to Jerusalem to visit his father, takes the Ark of the Covenant from the temple by the exercise of cunning and takes it back to Ethiopia, thus transferring the very legitimacy of the Davidic monarchy to that country.[1] And in fact, shortly afterwards the kingdom of Israel was to be divided into the two kingdoms of Judah and Samaria.

4.3 In Europe the narrative cycle known as the *Legend of the Wood of the Cross* is first recorded in written form in France towards the end of the second third of the 12th century; the first to expound it were Peter Comestor and John Beleth.[2] However, the cycle refers back to apocryphal and parabiblical works from the 1st centuries of the Christian era,[3] tracing the sacred wood all the way back to the seed Seth planted on the grave of his father Adam. The legend concludes with the triumphal return of the Cross to Jerusalem on 14 September 629, after fifteen years' captivity in Persia, where it had been confiscated by the Sasanian King

---

[1] Cf. Bezold *Kebra Nagast*; Cerulli *Letteratura*, 36-42; Cerulli *La regina*, 91.

[2] Cf. Petrus Comestor seu Manducator, *Historia scolastica. Liber III regum,* ch. 26, in *PL* 198, 1370; Joannes Belethus, *Rationale divinorum officiorum,* ch. 151, *De exaltatione sanctae crucis,* in *PL* 202, 152-153. Thus far, the critics have held that the association of the Queen of Sheba with the legend of the Cross was the fruit of the creative imagination of the mediaeval west, cf. Herr *La Reine*, 20.

[3] See above, notes 1-3, p. 46.

Khosraw II Parvīz.[1]

In this vast range of events, Solomon's meeting with the Queen of Sheba is re-established as a self-contained episode, after further elaboration and adaptation. The best description is that of Jacopo da Varazze,[2] in the 13th-century *Legenda Aurea*.[3] Briefly, the story as he tells it is this:

> When the Queen of Sheba arrived in Jerusalem, she hastened to Solomon's palace. On the way she had to cross a stretch of still water, from bank to bank of which a cedar trunk had been laid as an improvised bridge: this huge tree would otherwise have found no other employment. It had been cut down shortly before by order of King Solomon, and for all the carpenter's care in cutting it to the right length it was always either too long or too short for his purpose. It was the tree Seth had planted.
>
> When she found herself before this uncooperative length of wood the Queen was moved by an impulse to kneel down and worship it. An inner voice told her that on that very tree the Saviour of the world would hang. As soon as she told the King of this prophecy, Solomon had it removed to the most unexpected place: he had it buried at the bottom of the pool.
>
> Shortly before the Passion of Christ, the tree emerged unexpectedly from the bottom of this pool, which had meanwhile become the Sheep Pool.[4] Seeing it floating there and thinking that it would make a suitable upright for a cross, the High Priest's servants pulled it out of the water and delivered it to their master.

---

[1] From 614 to 628 the Cross was kept by the Zoroastrian clergy in the holy city of Shīz in Iranian Azerbaijan, cf. Ringbom *Paradisus*, 387-392.

[2] Jacopo da Varazze, who was born between 1228 and 1230, and died in 1298, was a Genoan Dominican who was Superior General of the Order of Preachers from 1283 to 1285 and Bishop of Genoa from 1292 to the year of his death.

[3] Ch. lxviii, *De inventione sanctae crucis*. See the Italian translation by Vitale Brovarone *Legenda*, 380-381.

[4] The name Probatica, given to the pool by Latin and, in general, western tradition, is the result of a punctuation error in *John* 5:2: '*Est autem Hierosolymis, super Probatica, piscina, quae cognominatur Hebraice Bethsatha.*' 'Probatica' refers here not to the pool, but to the Temple gate known in Greek as προβατική, 'of the sheep', near which the pool of Bethsatha or Bethesda was situated.

5. The Queen as seen by Piero della Francesca

The most famous pictorial representation of the tale is certainly the cycle of frescoes painted from 1452 to 1459 by Piero della Francesca in the church of St Francis, Arezzo, on the walls of the apse.[1] The Queen of Sheba is shown in middle register, in two scenes within the same panel on the right-hand wall.

Halfway along on the left the Queen is seen kneeling in adoration before a huge tree trunk which lies across a stream in open country. Around her, in silent astonishment, stand her ladies-in-waiting, while the grooms wait with the horses in the background to one side. Halfway along the right-hand section is shown the meeting of the two sovereigns in Solomon's magnificent palace.

It is clear that both Piero della Francesca and his predecessors chose not to follow the account of the *Legenda Aurea* as regards the water bridged by the beam. The *Legenda Aurea* explicitly states that the beam was laid across a stretch of water[2] in the city of Jerusalem, and that in that very place,[3] at a later date, the miraculous pool was situated.

In the same middle section, but on the back wall of the choir, to the right of the narrow Gothic window, is the scene of the 'transportation of the sacred wood'. Three workers are laboriously moving the heavy beam, which they have just taken out of the

---

[1] In point of fact, like his predecessors Agnolo Gaddi (1304) on the walls of the apse of Santa Croce in Florence, and his pupil and imitator Cenni di Francesco Cenni (1410) in the Oratory of the *Compagnia della Croce di Giorno* adjoining the church of San Francesco in Volterra, Piero della Francesca (c.1420-1492) brought together in a single cycle the various stages of the Invention and Exaltation of the Holy Cross. The latter ends with the victory of the Byzantine Emperor Heraclius over Khosrow II and the return of the Cross to Jerusalem. On the fortunes of the story of Solomon's meeting with the Queen of Sheba in figurative art from the 14th to the 16th century, see Herr *La Reine*.

[2] Jacopo da Varazze writes '*super quendam lacum*' (cf. Maggioni *Legenda Aurea*, 460), which in 14th-century Italian translations was rendered '*in su n' aquicella*', *i.e.* 'on a stream'. To this stream the name of Siloam is sometimes given, thus permitting the pool where the man born blind was healed (*John* 9:7, 11) to sneak into the story too.

[3] '*Postea probatica piscina ibidem facta est*', cf. Maggioni *Legenda Aurea*, 460.

pool.

There is no image of the trunk floating,[1] nor of the Queen wading across the stream because she will not set foot on the walkway.[2]

6. The floating tree trunk

It is my view that the Latin version of the story of the Queen of Sheba merges and mutually integrates three distinct motifs: (a) one which is common to the Jewish and Islamic traditions; (b) one which is inferred from the Byzantine tradition, and (c) one which is found only in the Jewish tradition.

The first, shared by all the Jewish and Islamic versions and taken over by the Coptic and Latin Christian versions, is the idea of a stretch of water which must be crossed so that the Queen and Solomon may meet, though close enough to recognise each other. It is true that in the Jewish and Islamic versions the stretch of water is really an illusion, but this circumstance is of negligible significance.

It is the Byzantine tradition that offers the cue to presenting the Queen of Sheba as an inspired woman with the gift of prophecy: like the sibyl Sabbe, she foresees the passion and death of Jesus, 'son of David'. It is no mere chance that John Beleth calls the Queen "Saba", exactly as in the *Testament of Solomon*.[3]

What is exclusively Christian, in that it is missing from the other versions, is the motif of the 'floating tree trunk'. In the Coptic legend it is represented by the heavenly, miraculous tree which is dropped on Jerusalem by the *rukh* and is floating on the esplanade of the temple when the queen arrives, whereas in the Latin legend it is the cedarwood beam which on the eve of the Crucifixion suddenly emerged from the bottom of the Sheep Pool,

---

[1] The scene of the workers pulling the trunk out of the miraculous pool was painted by Agnolo Gaddi in Santa Croce in Florence, and by Cenni di Francesco Cenni in San Francesco, Volterra.

[2] A representation of the queen wading through the stream alongside the footbridge was found in a wood print made by Boec van den Houte, published in 1483 (Herr *La Reine*, 12, Fig. 7) and in a fresco from the same century in the church of St Barbara in Hora-Kuttana, formerly Kuttenberg, in Bohemia (*ibid*., 16, Fig. 10).

[3] Cf. Belethus, *Rationale,* in *PL* 202, 153: '*regina Saba*'; McCown *Testament* , 64*, xxi, 1: καὶ Σάβα ἡ βασίλισσα Νότου.

breaking the surface of the water with a burst of waves, foam and splashes. This is what Jacopo da Varazze says; in contrast, Beleth holds that the pool *tempore passionis Christi desiccata fuit*, so the wood of the tree appears on the dry bed of the pool.[1] The evocative image of the trunk suddenly appearing in the middle of a stretch of water may have been prompted by the nineteenth riddle which one Jewish text puts into the mouth of the Queen of Sheba.[2] I refer to the trunk which is thrown into a pool of water, sinks and re-emerges, one end protruding from the water:

> XIX. The Queen then ordered a trunk sawn from a cedar to be brought to her and asked Solomon to show her which end had borne the roots and which the branches. He told her to throw it into the water, whereupon one end sank but the other remained on the surface. The part which sank corresponded to the roots and the part which stayed up corresponded to the branches...[3]

The nineteenth riddle may have sparked the imagination of an unknown Latin writer from the late ancient or mediaeval period, giving him the idea for a further episode to enrich the fascinating story of the *Legend of the Wood of the Cross*. How this motif reached the Latin west remains a mystery.

There is a sense in which the Queen of Sheba became the precursor of another famous queen, St Helena. Just as the mother of Constantine the Great found the wood of the Cross some centuries after the death of Christ, so the Queen of Sheba is supposed to have found it almost 1000 years before. This would in part bridge the enormous temporal gap between the death of Adam, on whose grave the first shoots of the holy Tree sprang up, and the Crucifixion of Christ, the heart of salvation history. The 'invention' of the Cross, its recovery from the hands of the Persians and its restitution to the Holy Sepulchre thus represent the final chapters of a very wide-ranging tale.

---

[1] Cf. Vitale Brovarone *Legenda*, 381; Belethus, *ibid.*

[2] The Queen of Sheba's nineteenth riddle is the last of a series of riddles recorded in the *Midrāš ha-ḥèfeṣ*, a Yemenite work which seems to reflect very ancient rabbinic sources. The setting of the riddle suggests that the first meeting of the Queen of Sheba with Solomon and the lively exchange of questions and answers between them took place at the edge of a pool near the palace or annexed to it.

[3] Cf. Schechter *The Riddles*, 355-356.

7. Solomon's grotto and the hoopoe devil

From the Gospel of St John, 5:1-18, in the episode of the paralysed man miraculously healed by Jesus, we learn that in Jerusalem, close to the gate of the Temple known as the Sheep Gate, there was a pool with five porticos.[1] Indeed, in 1914 an archaeological dig brought to light an immense reservoir filled with earth, divided into two basins by a stone dam running east to west.[2] As to the name of this pool, the Greek manuscripts show uncertainty, transcribing in various ways a single Judaeo-Aramaic name. It was probably called the pool of Beṣa'thā ('cleft, fissure') or Bēth Ḥesdā (Bethesda: 'house of mercy').

In the first case, the name would refer to the rocky ridge marking the eastern limit of the pool, and characterised by natural caves.[3] In the second case, the name would allude to a sort of therapeutic sanctuary alongside the most important[4] of these natural caves, and reached by crossing the dam.[5] Here there is a circular reservoir of modest size, surrounded by small pools with steps leading into them.[6] It seems to have been a public estab-

---

[1] *John* 5:2-3: '(2) Now in Jerusalem next to the Sheep Gate there is a pool called Bethesda in Hebrew, which has five porticos; (3) and under these were crowds of sick people, blind, lame, paralysed.'

[2] The two basins, carved out of the rock, are in the form of trapezoidal rectangles measuring together 4,650 m^2 (93 × 35/65 m), more than four times as large as an Olympic pool (50 × 21 m). See the chart in Alliata *Topografia*, 31 and Cohn *New ideas*, map C2. The dam separating the basins is approximately 40 m long and 6.5 m wide. The pool, of a depth greater than 8 m, received the water destined to the Temple. It appears to have been built by the high priest Simon II the Just, son of Onias II (220-195 BC), as stated in *Ecclesiasticus* 50:3. It may be, however, that King Hezekiah (716-687 BC) excavated the so-called 'upper pool' in the same area, see *2 Kings* 20:20; *Isaiah* 7:3; 36:2. As to the five porticos, no trace has been found of them, apart from the bases of a few pillars in the area east of the pool, cf. Del Verme *La piscina*, 111-112.

[3] Josephus Flavius (*Bell. Iud.* ii, 328, 530; v, 148, 151, 246: Βεζεθά) says that the entire hill and its village bore the same name, cf. Cohn *New ideas*, 32, 125.

[4] Cf. Del Verme *La piscina*, 112-113.

[5] Cf. Cohn *New ideas*, 30-32, 125.

[6] Cf. Testa *Maria*, 2.

lishment for hydrotherapeutic practices, and was used in three stages: a Jewish phase, a first Judaeo-Christian phase; a pagan phase linked to the healing god Asclepius or Serapis; and finally a second Judaeo-Christian phase (3rd-4th centuries AD).

In addition, St John's Gospel tells us that in Jesus' time sick people of all kinds would crowd under the porticos of this building[1] waiting to be healed by means of specific immersion rituals. It was in fact believed that from time to time an angel of the Lord came down into the pool and disturbed its waters: the first sick person to plunge into the water at that moment would be healed of any disease.[2]

Furthermore, the anonymous pilgrim from Bordeaux who visited Jerusalem in 333-334 AD tells us that the water in this public pool was reddish in colour and that this was also the site of the grotto where Solomon had tormented the devils.[3] As a matter of fact popular tradition related that it was in one of the natural caves of Bethesda that Solomon had subjugated the dark powers to whom he entrusted the building of the Temple. The *Testament of Solomon* recounts the capture and enslavement of these devils at some length.

With the Edict of Milan (313) and the building of the magnificent complex of the Holy Sepulchre[4] by Constantine (d. 337),

---

[1] Eusebius of Caesarea maintained that by 330 AD the porticos of Bethesda no longer existed, cf. Del Verme *La piscina*, 115. However, the Bordeaux pilgrim claimed to have seen them in 333-334; see note 3, *infra*.

[2] *John* 5:4: 'for at intervals the angel of the Lord came down into the pool, and the water was disturbed, and the first person to enter the water after this disturbance was cured of any ailment from which he was suffering'. This verse, which refers to a popular rumour confirmed by v. 7, is found in some secondary manuscripts of the Gospel of John, cf. Del Verme *La piscina*.

[3] Geyer *Itinerarium*, 21: '*interius vero civitati sunt piscinae gemellares, quinque porticos habentes, quae appellantur Betsaida. Ibi aegri multorum annorum sanabantur. Aqua(m) autem habent hae piscinae in modum coccini turbatam. Est ibi et crepta, ubi Solomon daemones torquebat.*' The mention of reddish water suggests that in ancient times there was a spring of iron-tasting mineral water in the site.

[4] Cf. Corbo *Il Santo Sepolcro*. The Constantinian constructions comprised, from east to west, a porch, a basilica with five naves called the *Martyrion*, a paved courtyard with three porticos and the round

Jerusalem became the official spiritual centre of an ecumenical Church which by that time consisted for the most part of believers of Gentile origin. As a result the space set aside for the therapeutic practices of the Judaeo-Christians – practices viewed with suspicion and haughty disdain by the ecclesiastical hierarchy of the time[1] – was progressively reduced until the Solomonic grotto was closed and the objects venerated there, first and foremost 'King Solomon's ring', were transferred to the recently built Holy Sepulchre. The pilgrim Etheria, who visited Jerusalem about the year 383, recounts that the magic ring was still being presented every Good Friday to be kissed by the crowd.[2] In the 5th century the Church of the Paralytic was built on the site of the healing baths.[3]

For a long time, then – certainly from the period of the Maccabees[4] until the second half of the 4th century AD – there was beside the pool of Bethesda the site of a therapeutic cult linked to the figure of Solomon and to his power over those devils who brought disease. This is confirmed by the many Solomonic amulets from the Roman period found in Jerusalem and in various parts of Palestine.[5] The connection between the Solomonic cult and the healings related in John 5:2-4,7 seems clear.

That said, it is not surprising that in all the versions – Jewish, Islamic and Christian – of the legend of the Queen of Sheba there should be the motif of the real or supposed stretch of water which the queen had to cross in order to reach the king. According to the *Targūm Shenī* it is the wet, sparkling surface of Solomon's baths;

---

church known as the *Anastasis*, its drum having a conic dome, in the centre of which rose the chapel of the Holy Sepulchre. This group of buildings covered the whole area of the sacred enclosure of the *Capitolium* of Aelia Capitolina (135 AD).

[1] Cf. Testa *Maria*, 16.

[2] Cf. Bagatti *Altre medaglie*, 341-342; Testa *Maria*, 17, note 63. The veneration of Solomon's ring on Good Friday was one way of affirming that Christ had defeated the powers of evil with his death, cf. Manns *L'Israel*, 161.

[3] Cf. Testa *Maria*, 17-20. The church of the Nativity of Mary was just next to the crypt of the present church of St Anne, built by the Crusaders.

[4] Judging by the coins and ceramics found in the excavations, cf. Testa *Maria*, 2. The Solomonic grotto may, however, have accommodated a popular cult even before the great pool was dug out at the beginning of the 2nd century BC.

[5] Cf. Bagatti *Altre medaglie*, 331; Nordio *Il sole*.

according to the Koran it is a shiny glass floor; according to the Arabic-language Coptic tale it is the Temple esplanade flooded by Solomon; finally, according to the *Legenda Aurea* it is the stretch of water (*lacus*) crossed by a small bridge where the miraculous pool was later located (*postea probatica piscina ibidem facta est*), and from which the wood of the Cross was to emerge. What seems to me to underlie all these representations is the indistinct memory of the rocky bathing sanctuary of the 'House of Mercy' with its five porticos and, in front of it, the pool crossed by a dam. This is where Solomon's victory over Onokolis 'the donkey-legged' was celebrated. It is, moreover, in the nature of things that such an outstanding woman as the Queen of Sheba should be confused with this evil female figure.[1]

We turn now to the hoopoe mentioned in the Jewish and Islamic versions of the legend. It is a mysterious creature, which can fly in the wink of an eye all the way across Arabia as far as the outer limit of the kingdom of Sheba, scanning everything as it goes.[2] I consider it useful to consult the *Testament of Solomon* in order to understand what it signifies:[3] in fact, this bird may be a

---

[1] The biblical episode concerning the meeting between Solomon and the Queen of Sheba might reflect a true historical fact. However, this episode should not be referred to the age of Solomon (10th century BC), but instead to the age of another king of Judah, one called Azariah, alias Uzziah (8th century BC). As a matter of fact the first documents regarding the incense trade from Arabia reach back to this age. On the other hand, king Azariah joined the coalition against the Assyrians, a coalition which was also supported by some Arab queens mentioned in Assyrian royal chronicles. We cannot exclude that one of these queens actually met his Hebrew ally in Jerusalem, where her presence might have left a lasting memory. This could interlace with an ancient popular legend connected with the building of the first Temple through Solomon and also with the magic-medical bathing sanctuary, possibly linked with Solomon's name. We should remember that Solomon was also considered to be a healer. Cf. Garbini *History*, 38-44 (*Azariah's misfortunes*); Pennacchietti *La via dell'incenso* 125, 131-132; Pennacchietti *Legends*, 33-34.

[2] Cf. *Koran* xxvii, 22: 'I have found out a thing that thou, Solomon, apprehendest not, and I come unto thee from Sheba with sure tidings.' *The Meaning of the Glorious Koran*, New York, undated.

[3] An esoteric-cabbalistic interpretation of the Koranic pericope regarding the hoopoe was proposed by Schedl *Sulaiman*, who saw in it links with the Iranian myth of King Yima and the bird Vāragan.

metamorphosis of the devil of an Arabian wind referred to in the Judaeo-Christian text.

Here the story is that Solomon, acting on behalf of a king of Arabia, calmed a violent wind which was ruining his kingdom. Solomon sent men to capture the devil which controlled this wind, and had it enclosed and 'sealed' in a leather flask. When it was brought to him in Jerusalem by camel, the king freed it from the flask and commanded it to move a huge cornerstone and place it in the Temple, for the stone could be moved by no other means.[1]

Now, the Greek text of the *Testament of Solomon* calls this devil *Ephippas*,[2] a personal name otherwise known as *Ephippos*, which means 'horseman'. My impression, however, is that *Ephippas* is simply an old adaptation of *Epopos*, a name which in Greek means 'hoopoe';[3] or, if the name *Ephippas* was the original form, it may have been confused with *Epopos*, a word not unknown in Aramaic-speaking communities.[4] In addition, three passages in the Koran[5] confirm that Solomon had power over a specific, particularly violent wind.

I maintain, therefore, that the oral tradition transformed the terrible Arabian wind (complete with its devil), called *Épops* or *Épopos*, into the hoopoe-messenger mentioned in texts in Hebrew, in Judaeo-Aramaic and in Arabic.

When Solomon asked *Ephippas* what angel had the power to resist him, the devil replied, 'He who will be born of a virgin and crucified...'.[6] Here, then, is another prophecy, like the Queen of

---

[1] Cf. Duling *Testament*, 983-985, chs. xxii-xxiv.

[2] Cf. McCown *Testament*, 26*, vi, 5; 68*, xxii, 19; 70*, xxiv, 1; variants Ἐφίππας, Ἐφιππάς, Ἐφιππᾶς, Ἔφιππας, Ἔφιππος, Ἐφήπτας.

[3] Greek ἔποπος, genitive of ἔποψ, 'hoopoe'.

[4] Cf. Syriac 'PWPWS 'hoopoe' < ἔποπος (Brockelmann *Lexicon*, 42b) and North-Eastern Neo-Aramaic *hāpūpkā* 'hoopoe', with the diminutive ending of Kurdish origin *-kā* (MacLean *Dictionary*, 78b).

[5] *Koran* xxi, 81: 'And unto Solomon (We subdued) the wind in its raging...'; xxxiv, 12: 'And unto Solomon We gave the wind, whereof the morning course was a month's journey and the evening course a month's journey...'; xxxviii, 36: 'So We made the wind subservient to him, setting fair by his command, whithersoever he intended' (*The Meaning of the Glorious Koran*, New York, undated).

[6] Cf. Duling *Testament*, 284, ch. xxii, 20.

Sheba's and the sibyl Sambethe's, one of the many heterogeneous motifs that interweave and intersect, involving Solomon in the history of the sacred wood of the Cross.

Moreover, there is a still earlier reference to the hoopoe as Solomon's messenger in the *Syriac Apocalypse of Baruch* (lxxvii, 25), an apocryphal work dating almost certainly from about 100 AD.[1]

8. Before and after Constantine

The name *Nikaulis* (< *Onokolis*) which Josephus attributes to the Queen of Sheba and the allusion in the *Syriac Apocalypse of Baruch* to the hoopoe's role of herald and messenger on Solomon's behalf lead to the probable conclusion that in the 1st century AD the legend of the Queen of Sheba was substantially similar to that reflected by the *Targūm Shenī* on the book of Esther.

Even the obvious differences between the two great narrative lines of the legend – the Jewish and Islamic on one hand, the Christian on the other – seem to lead back to the first centuries of the Christian era. It is my belief that the Jewish and Islamic versions, conforming as they do to the ideology and content of the *Testament of Solomon* (1st-3rd century AD) reflect the cultural and doctrinal climate dominant in Jerusalem before the Edict of Milan (313), in a period when it was the Judaeo-Christian current that prevailed in the Holy City.

In contrast, the Christian versions, both the Coptic and the Latin, which found its most complete expression only in the 13th century in Jacopo da Varazze's *Legenda Aurea*, seem to reflect the new spiritual and institutional orientation of Christianity in Jerusalem, leading to such memorable undertakings as the construction of the Church of the Holy Sepulchre by Constantine and the 'invention' of the Cross by his mother, St Helena. In this new cultural context it is easy to explain the insertion of the legend of the Queen of Sheba, as a prophetic tale, within the overall picture of the *Legend of the Wood of the Cross*. This is why, in cycles of mediaeval paintings, the queen appears not far from Constantine and Helena.

---

[1] Cf. Bettiolo *Apocalisse*, 226: 'Solomon too, during his reign, if he wanted to send (letters) somewhere or asked for something, gave orders to a bird and it obeyed him, according to his command.' This was indicated for the first time by Schedl (*Sulaiman*, 324).

But, despite the renewals promoted by Christian Gentiles obedient to the Emperor, the local Semitic element, both Jewish and Judaeo-Christian, continued undeterred to invent fables on the subject of the plot which demons are said to have contrived at the expense of a hirsute queen in the heterogeneous, colourful court of King Solomon. Echoes of this fabulous legend were in the end taken up and propagated *ad infinitum* in the sacred pages of the Book of Islam. Archaeologists have discovered that Hārūn ar-Rashīd, in imitation of Solomon, built a palace with glass floors.[1] Was he expecting the return of the Queen?

[1] Cf. Grabar *Essor*, 848, note 2. This is the Abbassid palace of ar-Raqqa, in Syria on the banks of the Euphrates (8th-9th century).

BIBLIOGRAPHY

AION = *Annali dall'Istituto Universitario Orientale di Napoli.*

B.H.G. = Halkin, F. (ed.), *Bibliotheca Hagiographica Graeca*, I-III, Brussells 1957: Société des Bollandistes.

B.H.L. = *Bibliotheca Hagiographica Latina antiquae et mediae aetatis ediderunt Socii Bollandiani*, Brussells 1898-1901.

B.H.O. = *Bibliotheca Hagiographica Orientalis ediderunt Socii Bollandiani*, Brussells 1910.

CIS = *Corpus Inscriptionum Semiticarum*, pars secunda, inscriptiones aramaicae continens, tomus III, fasc. I (Paris 1926); tabulae (Paris 1951).

CSEL = *Corpus Scriptorum Ecclesiasticorum Latinorum*, Prague-Vienna-Leipzig.

E.I.[1] = *Enzyclopaedie des Islâm*, I-IV, Leiden-Leipzig 1913-1934.

E.I.[2] = *Encyclopédie de l'Islam, nouvelle édition*, Leiden-Paris 1960-.

PG = J.-P. Migne, *Patrologia Graeca.*

PL = J.-P. Migne, *Patrologia Latina.*

Z.D.M.G. = *Zeitschrift der Deutschen Morgenländischen Gesellschaft.*

Adler-Seligsohn, *Chronique samaritaine* = Adler, E.-N. - Seligsohn, M., *Une nouvelle chronique samaritaine*, Paris 1903.

al-Antākī *Tazyīn al-aswāq* = al-Antākī, D., *Tazyīn al-aswāq fī akhbār al-'ushshāq*, Beirut s.d.: Dār wa-Maktabat al-Hilāl.

Albrile *Sethiani* = Albrile, E., "I Sethiani: una setta gnostica al crocevia tra Iran e Mesopotamia", *Laurentianum*, 37, fasc. 3 (1996), pp. 353-385.

Alliata *Topografia* = Alliata, E., *Topografia cristiana della Palestina. I. Gerusalemme e i dintorni,* Jerusalem 1988 (Studium Biblicum Franciscanum, n° 7).

Amir Khusrau *Le otto novelle del paradiso* = Amir Khusrau da Delhi, *Le otto novelle del paradiso*, Messina 1996: Rubbettino.

Arcangeli Marenzi *Tema della Vergine* = Arcangeli Marenzi, Maria Laura, *Aspetti del tema della Vergine nella letteratura francese del Medioevo*, Venice 1968: Libreria Universitaria Editrice.

Asín Palacios *Logia et agrapha* = Asín y Palacios, M., *Logia et agrapha Domini Jesu apud moslemicos scriptores, asceticos praesertim, usitata*, in "Patrologia Orientalis", t. XIII, fasc. 3, No. 64, Paris 1917 (reprint: Turnhout 1974), pp. 331-431.

Auboyer-Nou *Buddha* = Auboyer, J. - Nou, J.-L., *Buddha. Le chemin de l'Illumination*, Paris 1982: Seuil.

Bagatti *Altre medaglie* = Bagatti, B., "Altre medaglie di Salomone cavaliere e la loro origine", *Rivista di Archeologia Cristiana*, 47 (1971), pp. 331-342.

Battista-Bagatti *Caverna dei Tesori* = Battista, A. - Bagatti, B., *La Caverna dei Tesori. Testo arabo con traduzione e commento*, Jerusalem 1979 ("Studium Biblicum Franciscanum, Collectio Minor", No. 26).

Battista-Bagatti *Combattimento di Adamo* = Battista, A. - Bagatti, B., *Il combattimento di Adamo. Testo arabo inedito con traduzione italiana e commento*, Jerusalem 1982 ("Studium Biblicum Franciscanum, Collectio Minor", No. 29).

Bausani *Corano* = Bausani, A., *Il Corano. Introduzione, traduzione e commento di –*, Florence 1955.

Bausani *Letteratura neopersiana* = Bausani, A., "La letteratura neopersiana", in A. Pagliaro - A. Bausani, *La letteratura persiana*, Milan 1968: Sansoni, pp. 131-567.

Bausani *Persia religiosa* = Bausani, A., *Persia religiosa da Zaratustra a Bahâ'u'llâh*, Milan 1959: Il Saggiatore.

Bedjan *Vies des Saints* = Bedjan, P., *Vies des Saints*, Paris 1912 (in Neo-Aramaic).

Bernardini *Peregrinazioni letterarie* = Bernardini, M., "Peregrinazioni letterarie turco-iraniche della leggenda del Sultano Jomjome", in A. Pioletti - Francesca Rizzo Nervo (eds.), *Medioevo romanzo e orientale. Il viaggio dei testi*, Soveria Mannelli (CZ) 1999: Rubbettino, pp. 97-115.

Bertrand *La vie grecque d'Adam et Eve* = Bertrand, D.A., *La vie grecque d'Adam et Eve. Introduction, texte traduction et commentaire*, Paris 1987: Jean Maisonneuve.

Bettiolo *Apocalisse* = Bettiolo, P. (ed.), *Apocalisse siriaca di Baruc*, in P. Sacchi, *Apocrifi dell'Antico Testamento*, II, Turin 1989: UTET, pp. 147-233.

Bezold *Kebra Nagast* = Bezold, C., *Kebra Nagast. Die Herrlichkeit der Könige*, Munich 1905 (Abhandlungen der philos.-philol. Kl. der Kgl. Bayer. Akademie der Wissenschaften XXIII, 1).

Branca *Boccaccio medievale* = Branca, V., *Boccaccio medievale*, Florence 1970: Sansoni.

Branca *Decameron* = Branca, V. (ed.), *Giovanni Boccaccio, Decameron*, Turin 1980: Einaudi.

Bresciani *Antico Egitto* = Bresciani, Edda, *Letteratura e poesia dell'Antico Egitto*, Turin 1990: Einaudi.

Brockelmann *Lexicon* = Brockelmann, K., *Lexicon Syriacum*, Halle 1928.

Brüll *Susanna-Buch* = Brüll, N., 'Das apokryphische Susanna-Buch', *Jahrbücher für jüdische Geschichte und Literature*, 3 (1877), pp. 1-69.

Burton *Thousand Nights* = Burton, R.F., *The Book of the Thousand Nights and a Night*, I-XII, London 1894.

Busto Saiz *Interpretación del relato de Susana* = Busto Saiz, J.R., 'La interpretación del relato de Susana', *Estudios Eclesiásticos*, 57 (1982), pp. 12-30.

Canova *Bilqìs* = Canova, G. (ed.), *Tal'abi, Storia di Bilqìs regina di Saba*, Venice 2000: Marsilio.

Catastini *Susanna* = Catastini, A., "Il racconto di Susanna: riconsiderazioni di ipotesi vecchie e nuove", *Egitto e Vicino Oriente*, 11 (1988), pp. 195-204.

Cerulli *Letteratura* = Cerulli, E., *La letteratura etiopica*, Florence-Milan 1968: Sansoni-Accademia.

Cerulli *La regina* = Cerulli, E., "La regina di Sicilia e la regina di Saba in una tradizione dell'Egitto medievale", *Athenaeum*, 47 (1969), pp. 84-92.

Chabaneau *Romanz de Saint Fanuel* = Chabaneau, C., "Le Romanz de Saint Fanuel et de Sainte Anne et de Nostre Dame et de Nostre Segnor et de ses Apostres", *Revue des Langues Romanes*, 3e série, t. XIV (XXVIIIe de la collection), 1885, pp.

118-123, 157-258 (introduction et texte); 4e série, t. II (XXXIIe de la collection), 1888, pp. 360-409 (notes).
Chauvin *Bibliographie* = Chauvin, V., *Bibliographie des ouvrages arabes ou relatifs aux arabes publiés dans l'Europe chrétienne de 1810 à 1885.* VI. *Les Mille et une nuits (Troisième partie)*, Liège-Leipzig 1902.
Chauvin *Récension égyptienne* = Chauvin, V., *La récension égyptienne des Mille et une nuits*, Brussells 1899.
Chirassi Colombo *Gravidanze maschili* = Chirassi Colombo, I., "Giochi dell'immaginario greco: solipsismi spermatici, partenogenesi, gravidanze maschili", in M. Sbisà (ed.), *I figli della scienza*, Milan 1985, pp. 111-128.
Cohn *New ideas* = Cohn, E.W., *New ideas about Jerusalem's topography*, Jerusalem 1987: Franciscan Printing Press.
Corbo *Il Santo Sepolcro* = Corbo, V.C., *Il Santo Sepolcro di Gerusalemme*, Part I: *Text*; Part II: *Tables*; Part III: *Photographs*, Jerusalem 1981: Studium Biblicum Franciscanum.
Craveri *Vangeli apocrifi* = Craveri, M. (ed.), *I Vangeli apocrifi*, Turin 1969: Einaudi.
Crone-Cook *Hagarism* = Crone, Patricia - Cook, M., *Hagarism*, Cambridge 1977: Cambridge University Press.
Cunbur *Cimcime Sultan* - Cunbur, M., "Cimcime Sultan destanï", *Türk folkloru araştïrmalarï yïllïğï* (Ankara) 1976, pp. 40-54.
Cuneo *Le mura* = Cuneo, P., "Le mura di Derbent. Note sulla topografia e la morfologia urbana di una città-stato del limes islamico nell'area caucasica", in B.M. Alfieri - U. Scerrato (eds.), *Studi in onore di Ugo Monneret de Villard (1881-1954)*, II, *Il Mondo Islamico*, Rome 1987, pp. 57-75 (*Rivista degli Studi Orientali*, 59, 1-4, 1985).
D'Alverny *La connaissance* = D'Alverny, Marie-Thérèse, "La connaissance de l'Islam en Occident du IXe siècle", *L'Occidente e l'Islam nell'alto Medioevo, 2-8 April 1964*, II, Spoleto 1965, pp. 577-602.
de Goeje *Annales at-Tabari* = de Goeje, M.J. (ed.), *Annales quos scripsit Abu Djafar Mohammed Ibn Djarir at-Tabari (ta'rīkh ar-rusul wa-l-mulūk)*, I-XIII, Leiden 1879-1901.
de Menasce *Légende indo-iranienne* = de Menasce, J., "Une légende indo-iranienne dans l'angélologie judéo-musulmane: à propos de Hârût-Mârût", *Études asiatiques. Revue*

de la Société suisse d'études asiatiques, 1 (1947), pp. 10-18.

Deiana *Azazel in Lv. 16* = Deiana, G., "Azazel in Lv. 16', *Lateranum*, 54 (1988), pp. 16-33.

Del Lungo *Padri del deserto* = Del Lungo, I., *Leggende del secolo XIV*. I. *I Padri del deserto*, Florence 1863: G. Barbèra.

Del Verme *La piscina* = Del Verme, M., "La piscina probatica: *Gv.* 5: 1-9. Un problema di critica testuale e di esegesi di fronte ai risultati degli ultimi scavi", *Bibbia e Oriente*, 18 (1976), pp. 109-119.

Delatte *Anecdota* = Delatte, A., *Anecdota Atheniensia. Textes grecs inédits relatifs à l'histoire des religions*, I, Liège-Paris 1927.

Delcor *Le livre de Daniel* = Delcor, M., *Le livre de Daniel*, Paris 1971.

Delcorno *Modelli agiografici* = Delcorno, C., "Modelli agiografici e modelli narrativi. Tra Cavalca e Boccaccio", in *La Novella Italiana. Atti del Convegno di Caprarola. 19-24 settembre 1988*, Rome 1989: Salerno, pp. 337-363.

Delumeau *Storia del Paradiso* = Delumeau, J., *Storia del Paradiso. Il giardino delle delizie*, Bologna 1994: il Mulino (translation of *Une histoire du paradis. Le jardin des délices*, Paris 1992).

Dictionary of the Bible = *The Interpreter's Dictionary of the Bible*, I-IV, New York - Nashville 1962: Abingdon.

Dozy *Supplément* = Dozy, R., *Supplément aux dictionnaires arabes*, Leiden 1881.

Duchesne-Guillemin *Ancient Iran* = Duchesne-Guillemin, J., "The Religion of Ancient Iran", in C. Jouco Bleeker - G. Widengren (eds.), *Historia Religionum. Handbook for the History of Religions*, I, Leiden 1988, pp. 323-376.

Duling *Testament* = Duling, D.C. (ed.), *Testament of Solomon* in Charlesworth, J.H. (ed.), *The Old Testament Pseudepigrapha*, I, *Apocalyptic Literature and Testaments*, London 1983 [Vol. II, London 1985], pp. 935-987, translated text pp. 960-987.

Dumézil *Roman des jumeaux* = Dumézil, G., *Le roman des jumeaux et autres essais. Esquisses de mythologie. Vingt-cinq esquisses de mythologie (76-100) publiées par Joël H. Grisward*, Paris 1994: Gallimard.

Dussaud *Anciens bronzes* = Dussaud, R., "Anciens bronzes du Louristan et cultes iraniens (Pl. IX-X)", *Syria*, 26 (1949), pp. 196-229.

Engel *Die Susanna-Erzählung* = Engel, H., *Die Susanna-Erzählung. Einleitung, Übersetzung und Kommentar zum Septuaginta-Text und zur Theodotion-Bearbeitung*, Freiburg (CH)/Göttingen 1985.

Epstein *Sanhedrin* = Epstein, I. (ed.), *The Babylonian Talmud. Seder Nezikin.* III. *Sanhedrin*, London 1935: The Soncino Press.

Etienne *Thesaurus* = Etienne, *Thesaurus Grecae Linguae*, I-IV, Graz 1954.

Farīd ad-Dīn ʻAṭṭār *Elāhī-nāme* = Farīd ad-Dīn al-ʻAṭṭār, *Il Poema celeste*, Milan 1990: Biblioteca Universale Rizzoli.

Farīd ad-Dīn ʻAṭṭār *Tadhkirat al-Awliyā* = Farīd ad-Dīn al-ʻAṭṭār, *Parole di Sûfî* (titolo originale: *Tadhkirat al-Awliyā)*, Turin 1964: Boringhieri.

Ferdousī *Shāhnāme* = Ferdowsi, *The Epic of the Kings. Shah-Nama. The national epic of Persia, translated by Reuben Levy, revised by Amin Banani*, London 1977: Routledge and Kegan Paul ("Persian Heritage Series", 2).

Freedman-Simon *Midrash Rabbah* = Freedman, H. - Simon, M. (eds.), *Midrash Rabbah.* IV. *Leviticus*, 3rd edit., London - New York 1983: The Soncino Press.

Fritzsche-Grimm *Kurzgefasstes exegetisches Handbuch* = Fritzsche, O. - Grimm, C. (eds.) *Kurzgefasstes exegetisches Handbuch zu den Apokryphen des Alten Testaments*, Leipzig 1851, pp. 84-85.

Galland *Mille e una notte* = Galland, A., *Le mille e una notte*, I-IV, Novara 1964-1966: Istituto Geografico De Agostini.

Garbini *History* = Garbini, G., *History and ideology in ancient Israel*, London 1988: SCM Press.

García Martínez *Qumran and Apocalyptic* = García Martínez, F., *Qumran and Apocalyptic. Studies on the Aramaic Texts from Qumran*, Leiden 1992: E.J. Brill.

García Martínez *Testi di Qumran* = García Martínez, F. (ed.), *Testi di Qumran, Traduzione italiana dai testi originali con note di Corrado Martone*, Brescia 1996: Paideia.

Gaster *Daughter of Amram* = Gaster, M., "The story of the daughter of Amram: the Samaritan parallel to the apocryphal story of Susanna", in M. Gaster, *Studies and Texts in*

Folklore, Magic, Medieval Romance, Hebrew Apocrypha and Samaritan Archaeology, I-III, London 1925-1928 (reprint: Ktav Publishing House, New York 1971), pp. 199-210.

Gaster *Jerahmeel* = Gaster, M., *The Chronicles of Jerahmeel, or the Hebrew Bible Historiale being a collection of apocryphal and pseudo-epigraphical books dealing with the history of the world from the creation to the death of Judas Maccabeus*, 2nd edit., New York 1971.

Geissen *Susanna, Bel et Draco* - Geissen, A., *Der Septuaginta-Text des Buches Daniel Kap. 5-12, zusammen mit Susanna, Bel et Draco sowie Esther Kap. 1,1a-2,15 nach dem Kölner Teil des Papyrus 967*, Bonn 1968 ("Papyrologische Texte und Abhandlungen", 5).

Geyer *Itinerarium* = Geyer, P. (ed.), "Itinerarium Burdigalense", *CSEL*, XXXIX (1898), pp. 1-33.

Ginzberg *Legends* = Ginzberg, L., *The Legends of the Jews*, IV, Philadelphia 1968.

Grabar *Essor* = Grabar, O. & A., *L'essor des arts inspirés par les cours princières à la fin du premier millénaire: princes musulmans et princes chrétiens*, in *L'Occidente e l'Islam nell'Alto Medioevo. 2-8 April 1964*, II, Spoleto 1965, pp. 845-892.

Graf *Leggenda* = Graf, A., "Un testo provenzale della leggenda della croce", *Giornale di Filologia Romanza* (E. Monaci, Roma), 4, 1-2 (1882-1883), pp. 99-104.

Graf *Miti* = Graf, A., *Miti, leggende e superstizioni del Medioevo*. I. *Il mito del paradiso terrestre. Il riposo dei dannati. La credenza nella fatalità*, Turin 1892 (1st ed. 1882).

Graf *Un testo* = Graf, A., "Un testo provenzale della leggenda della croce", *Giornale di Filologia Romanza*, 4, 1-2 (1882-1883), pp. 99-104.

Graffin-Nau *Le synaxaire arabe-jacobite* = Graffin, R. - Nau, F., *Le synaxaire arabe-jacobite, rédaction copte*, in "Patrologia Orientalis", III, fasc. 3, No. 13, Turnhout 1982.

Graffin-Nau *Le synaxaire éthiopien* = Graffin, R. - Nau, F., *Le synaxaire éthiopien*, in "Patrologia Orientalis", XV, fasc. 5, Paris 1927.

Grossfeld *Targum Sheni* = Grossfeld, B. (ed.), *The Targum Sheni of Esther*, in *The Two Targums of Esther, translated, with*

Apparatus and Notes, Edinburgh 1991 (The Aramaic Bible, 18), pp. 95-201.

Grottanelli *Aspetti del sacrificio* = Grottanelli, C., "Aspetti del sacrificio nel mondo greco e nella Bibbia ebraica", in C. Grottanelli - N.F. Parise (eds.), *Sacrificio e società nel mondo antico*, Rome-Bari 1993: Laterza, pp. 123-162.

Grünbaum *Sagenkunde* = Grünbaum, M., *Neue Beiträge zur semitischen Sagenkunde*, Leiden 1893.

Grünbaum *Vergleichende Mythologie* = Grünbaum, M., "Beiträge zur vergleichenden Mythologie aus der Hagada", *Z.D.M.G.*, 31 (1877), pp. 183-359.

Harf-Lancner *Morgana e Melusina* = Harf-Lancner, L., *Morgana e Melusina. La nascita delle fate nel Medioevo*, Torino 1989: Einaudi (translation of *Les fées au Moyen Age. Morgane et Mélusine. La naissance des fées*, Paris 1984: Champion).

Henning *Book of the Giants* = Henning, W.B., "The Book of the Giants", *Bulletin of the School of Oriental and African Studies*, 11 (1943-1946), pp. 52-74.

Herr *La Reine* = Herr, J.L., "La Reine de Saba et le bois de la croix", *Révue Archéologique*, 23 (1914), pp. 1-31.

Hertz *Die Rätsel* = Hertz, W., "Die Rätsel der Königin von Saba", *Zeitschrift für deutsches Altertum und deutsche Literatur*, 27 (1883), pp. 1-33.

Histoire littéraire de la France = *Histoire littéraire de la France où l'on traite de l'origine et du progrès, de la décadence et du rétablissement des Sciences parmi les Gaulois... par des religieux bénédictins de la Congrégation de St. Maur*, XVIII, Paris 1895.

Hopkins *Early Arabic* = Hopkins, S., *Studies in the grammar of early Arabic based upon papyri datable to before A.H. 300/A.D. 912*, Oxford 1984: Oxford University Press.

Hucher *Le Saint-Graal* = Hucher, E. (ed.), *Le Saint-Graal ou Le Joseph d'Arimathie, première branche des Romans de la Table ronde, publié d'après des textes et des documents inédits*, I-III, Le Mans 1874 (reprint: Slatkine Reprints, Genève 1967).

Iacobini *L'albero della vita* = Iacobini, A., "L'albero della vita nell'immaginario medievale: Bisanzio e Occidente", in A.M. Romanini - A. Cadei (eds.), *L'architettura medievale in Sicilia: la cattedrale di Palermo*, Rome 1994, pp. 241-290.

Janssen *Bâbil, the City of Witchcraft* = Janssen, Caroline, *Bâbil, the City of Witchcraft and Wine. The name and fame of Babylon in medieval Arabic geographical texts*, Gent 1995 ("Mesopotamian History and Environment", Series I, Memoirs II).

Khoury *Codification* = Khoury, R.G., "Importance de 'Abd Allâh ibn Lahī'a (97-174/715-790), juge d'Égypte, et de sa bibliothèque privée dans la codification et diffusion des livres des deux premiers siècles islamiques", in Ahmed-Chouqui Binebine (ed.), *Le manuscrit arabe et la codicologie*, Rabat 1994 (Université Mohammed V, Publications de la Faculté des Lettres et des Sciences Humaines), pp. 105-114.

Khoury *Kalif, Geschichte und Dichtung* = Khoury, R.G., "Kalif, Geschichte und Dichtung: Der jemenitische Erzähler 'Abīd Ibn Sharya am Hofe Mu'āwiyas", *Zeitschrift für arabische Linguistik*, 25 (1993), pp. 204-218.

Khoury *Légendes prophétiques* = Khoury, R.G., *Les légendes prophétiques dans l'Islam depuis le Ier jusqu'au IIIe siècle de l'Hégire d'après le manuscrit d'Abū Rifā'a 'Umāra b. Wathīma b. Mūsā b. al-Furāt al-Fārisī al-Fāsawī* Kitāb bad' al-khalq wa-qiṣaṣ al-anbiyā' *avec édition critique du texte*, Wiesbaden 1978: O. Harrassowitz.

Khoury *Mille et Une Nuits* = Khoury, R.G., "L'apport de la papyrologie dans la transmission et codification des premières versions des *Mille et Une Nuits*", in *Les Mille et Une Nuits contes sans frontière*, Toulouse 1994, pp. 21-33.

Khoury *Wahb b. Munabbih* = Khoury, R.G., *Wahb b. Munabbih. Teil 1. Der Heidelberger Papyrus PSR Heid Arab 23. Leben und Werk des Dichters. Teil 2. Faksimiletafeln*, Wiesbaden 1972.

La Barre *Muelos* = La Barre, W., *Muelos. A Stone Age superstition about sexuality*, New York 1984: Columbia University Press.

Lassner *Demonizing the Queen of Sheba* = Lassner, J., *Demonizing the Queen of Sheba: boundaries of gender and culture in postbiblical Judaism and medieval Islam*, Chicago 1993: University of Chicago Press.

Le Roux de Lincy *Légendes* = Le Roux de Lincy, A.-J.-V., *Le livre des légendes. Introduction*, Paris 1836.

Lechler *The Tree of Life* = Lechler, G., "The Tree of Life in Indo-European and Islamic Cultures", *Ars Islamica*, 4 (1937), pp. 370-416.

Levi Della Vida *Gesù e il teschio* = Levi Della Vida, G., "Gesù e il teschio", *Bilychnis. Rivista mensile di studi religiosi*, 22, 2-3 (1923), pp. 196-201; reprinted in Idem, *Aneddoti e svaghi arabi e non arabi*, Milan-Neaples 1959: R. Ricciardi, pp. 162-169.

Levi Della Vida *Vaticano* = Levi Della Vida, G., "Manoscritti arabi di origine spagnola nella Biblioteca Vaticana", in *Collectanea Vaticana in honorem Anselmi M. Card. Albareda*, Città del Vaticano 1962, pp. 133-189.

Libro della Scala di Maometto = *Il Libro della Scala di Maometto (Liber Scalae Machometi)*, traduzione di Roberto Rossi Testa, note al testo e postfazione di Carlo Saccone, Milan 1991.

Lommel *Vedische Skizzen* = Lommel, H., "Vedische Skizzen", in *Beiträge zur indischen Philologie und Altertumskunde Walther Schubring zum 70. Geburtstag dargebracht von der deutschen Indologie*, Hamburg 1951 ("Alt- und neu-indische Studien", No. 7).

Lupieri *Mandei* = Lupieri, E., *I Mandei. Gli ultimi gnostici*, Brescia 1993: Paideia.

MacLean *Dictionary* = MacLean, A.J., *Dictionary of the Dialects of Vernacular Syriac*, Oxford 1901.

Macuch *Vorgeschichte der Bekenntnisformel* = Macuch, R., "Zur Vorgeschichte der Bekenntnisformel *lā ilāha illā llāhu*", *Z.D.M.G.*, 128 (1978), pp. 20-38.

Maggioni *Legenda Aurea* = Maggioni, G.P. (ed.), *Iacopo da Varazze, Legenda Aurea. Edizione critica*, Tavernuzze, Florence 1998: Edizioni del Galluzzo.

Mahābhārata = van Buiten, J.A.B. (ed.), *The Mahābhārata. 3. The Book of the Forest*, Chicago-London 1975: The University of Chicago Press.

Mahdi *Alf Layla wa-Layla* = Mahdi, M., *The Thousand and one Night (Alf Layla wa-Layla) from the earliest known sources. Arabic text edited with introduction and notes*, I-III, Leiden 1984-1994.

Manns *L'Israel* = Manns, F., *L'Israel de Dieu. Essais sur le Christianisme primitif*, Jerusalem 1996 (Studium Biblicum Franciscanum, Analecta 42).

Massignon *Parole donnée* = Massignon, L., *Parole donnée*, Paris 1967: Éd. du Seuil.
McCown *Testament* = McCown, C.C., *The Testament of Solomon*, Leipzig 1922.
Meyer *Geschichte* = Meyer, W., "Die Geschichte des Kreuzholzes von Christus", *Abhandlungen der philos.-philol. Cl. der köniğ. bayerischen Akademie der Wissenschaften*, XVI. Band, Munich 1882, pp. 103-166.
Meyer *Notice* = Meyer, P., "Notice sur un manuscrit interpolé de la Conception de Wace...", *Romania*, 16 (1887), p. 232; idem, "Notice sur un manuscrit français appartenant au Musée Fitzwilliam (Cambridge)", *Romania*, 25 (1896), pp. 562-561.
Migiel *Beyond seduction* = Migiel, Marilyn, "Beyond seduction: a reading of the tale of Alibech and Rustico (*Decameron* III, 10)", *Italica*, 75, 2 (1998), pp. 161-177.
Milik *Books of Enoch* = Milik, J.-T., *The Books of Enoch. Aramaic Fragments of Qumrân Cave 4*, Oxford 1976.
Milik *Susanne à Qumrân* = Milik, J.-T., "Daniel et Susanne à Qumrân?", in M. Carrez - J. Doré - P. Grelot (eds.), *De la Torah au Messie. Études d'exégèse et d'herméneutique bibliques offertes à Henri Cazelles pour ses 25 années d'enseignement à l'Institut Catholique de Paris (Octobre 1979)*, Paris 1981: Desclée, pp. 337-359.
Molé *I mistici musulmani* = Molé, M., *I mistici musulmani*, Milano 1992: Adelphi (translation of *Les mystiques musulmans*, Paris 1965: Presses Universitaires de France).
Mombello *Noël du Séminaire d'Aoste* = Mombello, G., "Analyse philologique d'un noël conservé dans deux manuscrits du Grand Séminaire d'Aoste", in *Le culte et ses rites: des témoins manuscrits aux expressions de la dévotion populaire. Actes du Colloque international d'Aoste (2 et 3 avril 1993)*, Aoste 1994, pp. 169-213.
Monier-Williams *Sanskrit Dictionary* = Monier-Williams, M., *A Sanskrit English Dictionary*, Oxford 1993 (1st edit. 1899).
Moore *Daniel* = Moore, C.F., *Daniel, Esther and Jeremiah: The Additions. A New Translation with Introduction and Commentary*, in "The Anchor Bible" 44, New York 1977.
Moraldi *Apocrifi del Nuovo Testamento* = Moraldi, L. (ed.), *Apocrifi del Nuovo Testamento*, I-II, Turin 1971: UTET.
Mussafia *Sulla leggenda* = Mussafia, A., "Sulla leggenda del

legno della Croce", *Sitzungsberichte der kaiserlichen Akademie der Wissenschaften zu Wien. Phil.-hist. Cl.*, LXIII. Band, II. Heft, 1869, pp. 165-216.

Najm *Das biographische Lexikon* = Najm, M.Y. (ed.), *Das biographische Lexicon des Salāhaddīn Halīl Ibn Aibak as-Safadī*, Teil 8, Wiesbaden 1982 (in Arabic).

Nestle *Zur Königin von Saba* = Nestle, E., "Zur Königin von Saba als Sybille", *Byzantinische Zeitschrift*, 13 (1904), pp. 492-493.

Neẓāmī *Haft Peikar* = Neẓāmī, *Le sette principesse* (titolo originale: *Haft Peikar)*, introduzione e traduzione di Alessandro Bausani, Milan 1996: Biblioteca Universale Rizzoli.

Niese *Ant. Iud.* = Niese, B., *Flavii Iosephi Opera. Antiquitatum Iudaicarum libri vi-x*, II, Berlin 1955.

Nordio *Il sole* = Nordio, M., *Il sole e il nimbo in alcuni amuleti palestinesi di età romana*, AION, 36 (1976), pp. 133-141.

Nordio *Elementi biblici* = Nordio, M., *Elementi biblici e post-biblici nell'iconografia timuride*, in *Atti del III Convegno Internazionale sull'Arte e sulla Civiltà Islamica. 'Problemi dell'età timuride' (Venezia 22-25 Ottobre 1979)*, Venice 1980: Quaderni del Seminario di Iranistica, Uralo-Altaistica e Caucasologia dell'Università degli Studi di Venezia, pp. 75-90 + 4 Tables.

O'Leary *Saints of Egypt* = O'Leary, De Lacy, *The Saints of Egypt*, London - New York 1937: Church Historical Society (reprint: Amsterdam 1974: Philo Press).

Paolella *Rustico ed Alibech* = Paolella, A., "I livelli narrativi nella novella di Rustico ed Alibech romita del Decameron", *Revue Romane*, 13 (1978), pp. 189-205.

Pauly = Pauly, *Realencyclopädie der classischen Altertums-wissenschaft*, 2. Reihe, 19. Halbband, Munich 1972.

Pauly-Wissowa = Pauly-Wissowa, *Real-Encyclopädie der Classischen Altertumswissenschaft*, 2. Reihe, 2. Halbband, Stuttgart 1920.

Pennacchietti *Gesù e Bālwān* = Pennacchietti, F.A., "Gesù e Bālwān bin Ḥafṣ bin Daylam, il sultano risuscitato", in P. Branca - V. Brugnatelli (eds.), *Studi arabi e islamici in memoria di Matilde Gagliardi*, Milan 1995: Istituto Italiano per il Medio ed Estremo Oriente, Sezione Lombarda, pp. 145-171.

Pennacchietti *Il racconto di Giomgiomé* = Pennacchietti, F.A., "Il racconto di Giomgiomé di Faridoddìn Attàr e le sue fonti cristiane", *Orientalia Christiana Periodica*, 62 (1996), pp. 89-112., + 7 plates.

Pennacchietti *La via dell'incenso* = Pennacchietti, F.A., "La via dell'incenso e la regina di Saba", in *Andata e ritorno dall'Antico Oriente. Cultura e commercio nei bagagli degli antichi viaggiatori. Atti del Convegno Internazionale, Milano, 16 marzo 2002*, Milan 2002: Centro Studi del Vicino Oriente, pp. 123-135.

Pennacchietti *Legends* = Pennacchietti, F.A., "Legends of the Queen of Sheba", in St John Simpson (ed.), *Queen of Sheba. Treasures from Ancient Yemen*, London 2002: The British Museum Press, pp. 31-38.

Pennacchietti *Osservazioni* = Pennacchietti, F.A., "Osservazioni sui termini arabi, turchi e persiani resi in caratteri latini o registrati in scrittura originale", in A. Invernizzi (ed.), *Pietro Della Valle, In viaggio per l'Oriente. Le mummie, Babilonia, Persepolis*, Alessandria 2001: Edizioni dell'Orso, pp. 259-270.

Pennacchietti *San Giorgio* = Pennacchietti, F.A., "Il parallelo islamico di un singolare episodio della passione di San Giorgio", *Bollettino della Società per gli Studi Storici, Archeologici e Artistici della Provincia di Cuneo*, 107 (1992), pp. 101-110.

Pennacchietti *Teschio redivivo* = Pennacchietti, F.A., "La leggenda islamica del teschio redivivo in una versione neoaramaica", in G. Goldenberg - Sh. Raz (eds.), *Semitic and Cushitic Studies*, Wiesbaden 1994: Harrassowitz, pp. 103-132.

Pennacchietti *Versione neoaramaica* = Pennacchietti, F.A., "La versione neoaramaica di un poema religioso caldeo in lingua curda", in B. Scarcia Amoretti - L. Rostagno (eds.), *Yâd-Nâma in memoria di Alessandro Bausani*, II, Rome 1991: Bardi, pp. 169-183.

Pertsch *Gotha* = Pertsch, W., *Die arabischen Handschriften der herz. Bibliothek zu Gotha*, I-IV, Gotha 1878-1892.

Pfeiffer *History of the New Testament Times* = Pfeiffer, R.H., *History of the New Testament Times. With an Introduction to the Apocrypha*, New York 1949.

Philby *The Queen* = Philby, H. St.J., *The Queen of Sheba*, London

1981.

Ribezzo *Ibrido* = Ribezzo, F., "Di un ibrido italiota in Petronio: lat. *(o)clopeta*, nap. *lúppeca* 'upupa, gallo selvatico'", *Rivista Indo-greco-italica*, 14 (1930), pp. 106-108.

Ringbom *Paradisus* = Ringbom, L.-I., *Paradisus Terrestris. Myt, bild och verklighet*, Helsinki 1958 ('Acta Societatis Scientiarum Fennicae', Nova Series C., I, N° 1).

Rosso Ubigli *Apocalisse di Mosè* = Rosso Ubigli, Liliana (ed.), *Apocalisse di Mosè*, in P. Sacchi (ed.), *Apocrifi dell'Antico Testamento*, II, Turin 1989: UTET, pp. 417-446 (reprint: Florence, TEA, 1993, pp. 579-608).

Rosso Ubigli *Vita di Adamo ed Eva* = Rosso Ubigli, L. (ed.), *La Vita di Adamo ed Eva*, in P. Sacchi (ed.), *Apocrifi dell'Antico Testamento*, II, Turin 1989: UTET, pp. 447-471 (reprint: Florence, TEA, 1993, pp. 609-633).

Rudolph *Mandäer* = Rudolph, K., *Die Mandäer*. I. *Prolegomena: Das Mandäerproblem*, Göttingen 1960; II. *Der Kult*, Göttingen 1961.

Sacchi *Apocrifi* = Sacchi, P. (ed.), *Apocrifi dell'Antico Testamento*, I, Turin 1981: UTET.

Sacchi *Attesa* = Sacchi, P., "L''attesa' come essenza dell'apocalittica", in *Rivista Biblica Italiana*, 45 (1997), pp. 71-78.

Saccone *Il verbo* = Saccone, C. (ed.), *Farīd ad-Dīn 'Aṭṭār, Il verbo degli uccelli*, Milan 1986: SE Studio Editoriale.

Saintyves *Vierges Mères* = Saintyves, P., *Les Vierges Mères et les Naissances Miraculeuses. Essai de mythologie comparée*, Paris 1908.

Scarcia *Çemberlitaş, Monodendron, Ṣanoubar* = Scarcia, G., "Çemberlitaş, Monodendron, Ṣanoubar", *Gururājamañjarikā. Studi in onore di Giuseppe Tucci*, I, Napoli 1974, pp. 305-311.

Schechter *The Riddles* = Schechter, S., "The Riddles of Solomon in Rabbinic Literature", *Folk-Lore*, 1 (1890), pp. 349-358.

Schedl *Sulaiman* = Schedl, C., *Sulaiman und die Königin von Saba. Logotechnische und religionsgeschichtliche Unter-suchung zu Sure 27, 17-44*, in Roswitha G. Stiegner (ed.), *Al-Hudhud. Festschrift Maria Höfner zum 80. Geburtstag*, Graz 1981, pp. 305-324.

Schürer *Storia* = Schürer, E., *Storia del popolo giudaico al tempo di Gesù Cristo (175 a.C.-135 d.C.)*, Edition and revised by

G. Vermes, F. Millar, M. Goodman, III/1, Italian edition ed. C. Gianotto, Brescia 1997.

Schwarzbaum *Biblical legends* = Schwarzbaum, H., *Biblical and Extra-Biblical Legends in Islamic Folk-Literature*, Walldorf-Hessen 1982.

Schwarzbaum *Prolegomenon* = Schwarzbaum, H., "Prolegomenon" in M. Gaster, *The Chronicles of Jerahmeel*, 2nd edit., New York 1971, pp. 1-124.

Serjeant *Miḥrāb* = Serjeant, R.B., "Miḥrāb", *Bulletin of the School of Oriental and African Studies*, 22, 3 (1959), pp. 439-453.

Shepherd *Sasanian art* = Shepherd, Dorothy, "Sasanian art", in *The Cambridge History of Iran*, III/2, Cambridge 1983, pp. 1055-1112.

Stark *Personal Names* = Stark, J.K., *Personal Names in Palmyrene Inscriptions*, Oxford 1971.

Steingass *Persian-English Dictionary* = Steingass, F., *A Comprehensive Persian-English Dictionary*, London s.d.

Stenhouse *Falasha and Samaritan versions* = Stenhouse, P., "Further reflections on the Falasha and Samaritan versions of the legend of Susanna", in *Between Africa and Zion. Proceedings of the First International Congress of the Society for the Study of Ethiopian Jewry*, Ben-Zvi Institute, Jerusalem 1995, pp. 94-102.

Stiegner *Die Königin* = Stiegner, R.G, *Die Königin von Saba' in ihren Namen. Beiträge zur vergleichenden semitischen Sagenkunde und zur Erforschung des Entwicklungsganges der Sage*, Dissertationen der Universität Graz 44, Graz 1979.

Su-Min Ri *Caverne des Trésors* = Su-Min Ri (ed.), *La Caverne des Trésors. Les deux versions syriaques*, I-II, Louvain 1981.

Testa *Maria* = Testa, E., *Maria Terra Vergine*. II. *Il culto mariano palestinese (sec. I-IX)*, Jerusalem 1984: Studium Biblicum Franciscanum, Collectio Maior, n°. 31.

Thieme *Aryan gods* = Thieme, P., "The 'Aryan' gods of the Mitanni treaties", *Journal of the American Oriental Society*, 80 (1960), pp. 301-317.

Thompson *Motif-Index* = Thompson, S., *Motif-Index of Folk-Literature*, Copenhagen 1957.

Tottoli *Il rifiuto* = Tottoli, R., "La moderna esegesi islamica ed il rifiuto delle *Isrā'īliyyāt*: le leggende sul bastone di Mosè mutato in serpente", *Annali di Ca' Foscari* (Venice), s.o. 21 (1990), pp. 25-35.

Tottoli *Jesus and the skull* = Tottoli, R., "The story of Jesus and the skull in Arabic literature: the emergence and growth of a religious tradition", *Jerusalem Studies in Arabic and Islam*, 28 (2003), pp. 225-259.

Tottoli *Origin* = Tottoli, R., "Origin and use of the term *isrā'īliyyāt* in Muslim literature", *Arabica*, 46 (1999), pp. 193-210.

Trumpf *Alexander* = Trumpf, J., "Alexander und die Königin von Saba", *Atenaeum*, 44 (1966), pp. 307-308.

Venzlaff *Al-Hudhud* = Venzlaff, Helga, *Al-Hudhud: eine Untersuchung zur kulturgeschichtlichen Bedeutung des Wiedehopfs im Islam*, Frankfurt - New York 1994.

Vilmar *Abū l-Fatḥ* = Vilmar, E., *Abulfathi Annales Samaritani*, Gotha 1865.

Vitale Brovarone *Legenda* = Vitale Brovarone, A. and L. (eds.), *Iacopo da Varazze, Legenda Aurea*, Turin 1995.

Widengren *Iranisch-semitische Kulturbegegnung* = Widengren, G., *Iranisch-semitische Kulturbegegnung in parthischer Zeit*, Köln-Opladen 1960 ("Arbeitsgemeinschaft für Forschung des Landes Nordrhein-Westfalen, Gesteswissenschaften", Heft 70).

Widengren *Manichaeism* = Widengren, G., "Manichaeism and its Iranian background", in E. Yarshater (ed.), *The Cambridge History of Iran*, III (2), *The Seleucid, Parthian and Sasanian Periods*, Cambridge 1983, pp. 965-990.

Widengren *The King and the Tree of Life* = Widengren, G., *The King and the Tree of Life in Ancient Near Eastern Religion (King and Saviour IV)*, Uppsala 1951 ("Acta Universitatis Upsaliensis" 1951, No. 4).

Wurmbrand *Falasha Susanna* = Wurmbrand, M., "A Falasha Variant of the Story of Susanna", *Biblica*, 44, 1 (1963), pp. 29-45.

THE STORY OF THE SKULL AND THE KING

Arabic text (Ms. Gotha orient. A 2756, ff. 30a-44b)

[ص 30-آ]

حديث الجمجمة مع الملك[1]

بسم الله الرحمن الرحيم

قيل انّه كان في زمان ملك من ملوك بني اسرآيل ملك عظيم الشّان كثير الأعوان وكان مشهورًا بالايمان وعبادة الملك الديان قام على ذلك مدة من الزمان في أطيب عيش وأهناه وكان مشهوراً بالصّيد وكان يخرج الى الصيد فيقيم عشرة أيام وشهراً اذا أراد صيداً وانّه خرج ذات يوم من

---

[1] ملاحظة: إشارة <> = حرف واجب الحذف؛ إشارة # = حرف ممحو؛ إشارة [ ] = حرف واجب الإضافة

قصره وامر غلمانه بشدّ الدّواب واخرج الطعام
والفهود والبازات والبواشق والعقبان [ص 30-ب]
وسآير آلة الصيّد وسار الملك ومعه عسكره
وغلمانه ومعهم الكلاب السلاقية فسار يومه
ذلك وليلته فأصبح له الصّباح على أرض نقيّة
كأنّها فضة مجلية قليلة الحظر كثيرة النّبات
والشجر مشبكة الأغصان وحشيشها الزّعفران
وزهرها شقايق النعمان وعلى تلالها قضبان
الخيزران توقف الساير وتبهت العابر كثرة
انهارها وتدفق ميآتها فيها شجرة عالية الإنتها
وفيها سآير الأطيار من قمري وشحرور وبلبل
وفاخت وزرزور فطرب لها الملك طرباً شديداً
وأمر بالخيام فضُربت فيها ونُصبت الغارات [ص
31-آ] وتفرق القوم بين تلك الأشجار فقوم

يصطادون الطّير وقوم يصطادون السّمك في
تلك النهر وركبوا أصحاب الفهود وكانت
تلك [الأرض] كثيرة الضبّ والأرنب وبقر
الوحش فاصطادوا من ذلك شيء كثير فبعضهم
جاب السمك من ذلك الّنهر فاوقدوا النّيران
وأكلوا لحم الغزلان والسمك والطّير فقعد الملك
في تلك الأرض عشرة ايّام فلمّا كان ذات يوم
ركب الملك فرسا ## له يقال لها العُقاب وهو
حصان # أشقر كأنّ غرته صبح اذا اسفر كان
قوايمه من حديد أو حجر<ا> يمر كالبحر إذا
<ا>زخر ## او كريح اذا اغبر في خلقة
السرحان <الذيب> وسرعة [ص 31-ب] الغزلان
الطّير لا يدرك منتهاه ولا يرام لقاه وتقلد
بصفيحة هنديّة مشرقة مضية وقناة سمهريّة

ودرقة تنبتية ولبس خلعة نسبة وسار يتفرّج بين تلك الأشجار والحدايق فبينما هو كذلك إذ أبصر غزالة مليحة بيضا على ظهرها حلل ديباج وفي عنقها قلادة عنبر وعقد جوهر وفي أذنها جوهرتين كنار تضيء مثل الشمس فأبصرها الملك واستحسنها فقال هذه لا شك خرجت من دار ملك واطمعته نفسه في اخذها فهمز الفرس فخرج من تحته كانّه عقاب أو قطعة سحاب وجدّ في طلبها فانقطع منه العسكر وانفرد بنفسه من العسكر وكانت [ص 32-آ] الغزالة إذا أراد الملك <وقف> الوقوف وقفت تطمعه في نفسها وهو بكّر بالفرس خلفها إلى ان انتهت به إلى جبل عظيم وتحته كهف فدخلت الغزالة في ذلك الكهف فنزل الملك عن جواده ودخل الكهف

خلفها فلم يرا لها خبر ولا وقع لها على # اثر
واغتمّ غمّاً شديداً كيف اتعب نفسه وفرسه
فبينما هو كذلك يدور ذلك الكهف إذ# نظر
إلى جمجمة عظيمة نخرة لم ير أهول# منها
فجعل يقلّبها ويتعجّب من كبرها فقال يا ليت
شعري أي العذاب كان أشدّ على هذه
الجمجمة الدّود وصولته والقبر وضيقته وما
حُثي عليها [من] الثراب او عذاب جهنّم ولهيبه
[ص 32-ب] [و] النّيران ويا ليت شعري لمن كانت
هذه الجمجمة لملك أو لشريف او لدنيّ أو لعزيز
أو لذليل أو لغنيّ أو لفقير وبقي بتعجّب من كبرها
والحاجبين فتاه عقله وخاطر في ذلك قلبه
و<ا>دخل قلبه الشّرك بالله تعالى فقال اظنّ هذه
الجمجمة ما ترجع خلقاً كما كانت أبداً ولا

تأكل ولا تشرب وتتنعّم ولا تعذّب وأخذها معه
وحملها على جواده إلى أن لحق بأصحابه فبات
في ذلك الموضع متفكّراً فلمّا أصبح ركب وسار
الى المدينة ودخل القصر الذي له وطلب الحكما
الفلاسفة والعلما وجعل الجمجمة في طشت
ذهب واحضرها بين أيديهم وقال لهم ما تقولون
[ص 33-آ] يا معاشر الحكما في هذه الجمجمة
أترونها تعود كما كانت تاكل وتشرب وتلذّ
وتطرب او تعذّب أو تنعّم هذا ما يكون ولا
يتصوّر في الظنون فقالوا العلما مثل ذلك
و<ا>داخلهم الشكّ في الله تعالى ثم انّ الملك
طلب البستاني وقال له خذ هذه الجمجمة
وادّخـــ<ـيـــ>ـــرها عندك في البستان حتّي
أسالك عنها فاخذها البستاني ودخل بها إلى

البستان وحفر لها حفيرة ودفنها فيها وانشاها الله
عزّ وجلّ ### ايّلهاً وكذلك الملك فأراد الله
تبارك وتعالى ان يظهر معجزتها فانبت الله تعالى
في الجمجمة قضيباً وكبر ونشا وصار شجرة
عظيمة وحملت ثمرة في خلقت [ص 33-ب]
السّفرجل وطعم #### الكمترى فأقبل إليها
البستاني فنظر إلى الشجرة وتعجّب من خلقتها
وحُسنها وكان شيخ كبير فمدّ يده الى الشّجرة
فأخذ منها ثمرة فأكلها فأصابها أطيب ما يكون
فبعد ساعة سقط شعر رأسه ولحيته ورجع أمرد
ما في وجهه شعر ورجعت إليه قوّته كما كانت
في أوّل مرّة ثمّ مدّ يده إلى ثمرة أخرى فرجع
شابّ مليح بلحيته حسنة سودا مليحة فأخذ
صينيّة وجعل فيها ثلاث ثمرات وغطّاهنّ بمنديل

من حرير ودخل القصر إلى عند الملك فقالوا له البوّابين أيش انت فقال انا فلان البستاني فأدخلوه إلى الملك [ص 34-آ] وقال له الملك قُصّ على قصّتك وخبّرني بخبرك ومحنتك فأنت كنت شيخاً واليوم بقيت شابّ قال يا مولاءي طلع في البستان شجرة عالية البنا واسعة القنا لها أغصان كثيرة وهذا ثمرها فنظرها الملك وبقي يتعجّب منه عجباً شديداً ثمّ قال البستاني يا مولاءي أخذت واحدة من هذه الثّمرة فأكلتها فرميت شعر رأسي وقصّ عليه ما جرى له قال فأخذ الملك من ذلك الثمر واحدة وأكلها فازداد قوّة في حيله وقوة ### في بدنه وحسُن قلبه وحسُن بالقوة والصحّة والنشاط فأمر الملك أن يُبنى بجنب الشجرة محراباً وعلّق القناديل في الشّجرة ثمّ

طيّبوها [ص 34-ب] بأنواع الطيب وأصلح تحتها
الشّمع الكافوري توقد وأنذر لها النذور و#جعل
لها قيّماً فإذا اكل منها شيخاً رجع صبياً وان
اكل منها مريضاً يقوم ويصحّ من وقته ولو عمي
يبصر فحُملت إليها النذور العظيمة من كلّ
جانب ومكان ولم يبقى أحد إلاّ وحمل إليها
الطيب والشمع فسمعت إبنة الملك بالشجرة
كان إسمها الرّباب فقالت لأبيها يا أبت قد
اشتهيت أن أخرج إلى هذه الشجرة وأصلّي
عندها وأنذر لها نذراً فقال الملك للفرّاشين
اضربوا في البستان السّرادقات حول الشجرة
فضُربت وبُسطت #### السّرادقات بالبسط
فلمّا اصبح الصّباح خرجت [ص 35-آ] الجارية
وأمّها ودایاها وجواريها ومن يعزّ عليها

وحشمها وخدمها وتفرّجوا في البستان وأكلت الرّباب من أثمارها وأقبلت إلى الشّجرة وأبصرت ثمرها فاخذت منها ثمرة وأكلتها ولم تزل في البستان إلى غياب الشمس فاصرفت إلى قصرها فلمّا مضى لها يومين اصفرّ وجهها وكُبر بطنها وتغيّر لونها وازداد بها الأمر فنظرت إليها والدتها فأنكرت حالها فقالت يا إبنتي قُصّي عليّ قصّتكي وما الذي دهاكي يا إبنتي لا يكون قربك بشر قالت والله يا أمّي ما قرُبني بشر ولا لحقني شيء من الأمور إلاّ من وقت أكلت الثمرة [ص 35-ب] في البستان فلحقني ما تري فدخلت والدتها على الملك وهي متفكّرة فسلّمت عليه فردّ عليها السّلام وأمرها بالجلوس فجلست وحدّثت الملك بحديث إبنته الرّباب وما جرى لها فاغتمّ

الملك غمّاً شديداً لّما سمع هذا الحديث وقال عليّ بالجارية فصاحوا بها الجوار فأقبلت إليه وسلّمت عليه فقال يا إبنتي أصدقيني في حديثك وخبرك لا يكون أحداً من الأصحاب قربك بسوء قالت له مثل ما قالت لأمّها فقال الملك لوالدتها صيحي بالدّايات يبصروها فخرجت والدتها من عند الملك وبعثت خلف الدّايات فأقبلت إليها [ص 36-آ] فنظرت إلى الجارية فإذا هي بكر بخاتم ربّها عزّ وجلّ فاخبروا الملك بذلك فبقي يغوص في بحار الفكر ثمّ أنّه خرج إلى البستان وأقبل إلى الشجرة فنظرها وإذا هي بها قد اصفرّت وتغيّرت فأمر بإحضار القيّم الّذي في البستان وسأله عن الجمجمة فتفكّر وتحيّر ساعة زمانيه وحفر جانب الشجرة وظهرت الجمجمة والشجرة في وسط

يافوخ الجمجمة فعلم انّ الله تعالى أدرى الملك
قدرته في ابنته فخرج الملك إلى قصره واستحضر
العلما والحكما والفلاسفة الّذي دخل في قلوبهم
الشّك في الله عزّ وجلّ [ص 36-ب] فأدراهم
الجمجمة فتعجّبوا من ذلك وعلموا انّ الله على
كل شيء قدير ثمّ حملت الجارية الرّباب تسعة
أشهر فلحقها كرب عظيم وانشقّ جنبها الأيمن
من تحت اضلاعها فخرجت منه جارية مثل
الشّمس وماتت إبنـــ<ـــيـــ>ـــة الملك لوقتها
وساعتها فحزن الملك عليها حزناً شديداً وأمر
بتجهيزها ودفنها وبكا عليها الملك بكأ شديداً
فبينما هو جالس وأمرآيه حوله يعزّونه إذ دخل
البستاني وقال ايها الملك أحسن الله عزاك في
الشّجرة فقد يبست فتعجّب الملك ومن حضر

من أصحابه وعلم انّ الله جلّ ذكره وتقدّست
أسماؤه حكم عدل لا يجوزه <يفوته> شيء وأمر
الملك الدّايات والجوار [ص 37-آ] والمرضعات أن
يربوا الصّغيرة وسمّاها سَوسَنَه فلم تزل تربّى إلى
أن بقي لها من العمر اثناعشر سنة فدخلت على
الملك يوماً من الأيّام فسلّمت عليه فأمرها
بالجلوس فجلست [وسألت] من أبيها فحدّثها
الملك الحديث مع الجمجمة والشجرة وكيف
دخل قلبه الشكّ في الله تعالى وكيف اكلت إبنته
الثمر وعلقت بها وكيف خرجت من تحت
ضلوعها فاستعجبت العجب الشّديد وقالت
ايها الملك فمن خلقني من غير أب لا بدّ أن أعبده
وأسبّحه وأقدّسه وأمجّده وأعظّمه وقد اشتهيت
أن تبني لي ديراً وتغرز فيه من الأشجار وتبني فيه

صومعة عالية أعبد الله [ص 37-ب] فيها إلى حين
ألقاه قال وأمر الملك في الحال أن يُبنى لها ما
ذكرت فجمع الصنّاع من كلّ جانب ومكان
وبنا لها صومعة كما طلبت واشتهت فلبست
ثياب الصوف وانتقلت إلى الصّومعة والدّير
ونقل إليها الملك كلّما تحتاج من سآير الأشياإ
ووهب لها ثلاث جوار يخدمونها وهي تتلوا
الزّبور وكان لها صوت عظيم حسن ومن حُسن
صوتها وحسن نغمتها كانت الطيور يقف على
رأسها وكانوا جميع العبّاد يأتون إليها من سآير
النّواحي ويتعجّبون من حُسن صوتها وكان قُربها
دير عظيم فيه خلق كثير من العبّاد والزهّاد وإلى
جانب الدّير صومعة فيها [ص 38-آ] عابدين الواحد
يقال له هِرَم والأخر يقال له هُرَيم وقد عبدوا الله

عزّ وجلّ وعليهما من الحُسن والجمال وقرآت
الزّبور بالصّوت الحسن فنزلا ذات يوم من
صومعتهما وأقبلا ناحية الجارية وسلّما عليها
فقالت لهما الجارية بعد أن ردّت عليهما السّلام
ما الذي أنزلكما من صومعتكما أيها العابدان
الزّاهدان قالا نزلنا لافتقادك وسماع قرأتك
فقرأت عليهما الزبور فتعجّبا من ذلك وراحا إلى
صومعتهما ووقع في قلوبهما من الجارية ايقاع
عظيم وحبّوها حبّاً شديداً ولم يذكروا الله تعالى
بشفة ولا بلسان ودخل بينهما اللّعين إبليس فلمّا
اصبح هرم وهريم واجتمعا هما وابليس [ص 38-ب]
فقال هرم لهريم ما سمعت لك البارحه حسّ قرأة
ولا كلام فقال هريم وكذلك أنت ايضاً ما
سمعت لك قرأة ولا صلواة فما قصّتك فقال والله

يأخي لقد اخذت هذه الجارية من قلبي وخالط
حبّها بجوارحي فقال هرم وكذلك أنا والله
يأخي فما الحيلة أن نو#قِع هذه الجارية فقال
نمضي إليها انا وأنت ونقل لها انزلي إلينا فإذا
نزلت فعلنا بها الذي نريد فنزلا جميعاً من
صومعتهما وأتيا إلى صومعة سَوسَنَه وسلّما
عليها فردّت عليهما السّلام ورحّبت بهما فقالوا
لها يا سوسنه ما تنزلي إلى عندنا نتبرّك بطلعتك
السعيدة فنزلت إلى عندهما وأحضرت لهما
طعاماً [ص 39-آ] فأكلا منه وتحدّثت معهما ساعة
فاهتمّت بالقيام فقبضا عليها ومسكاها فقالت
لهما على أيّ شيء مسكتماني وأيّ شيء عزمتما
عليه قالا لها تمكّنينا من نفسك فقالت لهما سمعاً
وطاعة أما علمتما أنّي قد نصبت على الملك

حتّى بنا لي هذه الصّومعة وهذا الدير وخرجتُ
قعدتُ لأنّي قد وقع في قلبي منكما شيء فما تمّ
لي أمري حتّى <علمت> عملت هذه المكيدة
على الملك حتّي بنى لي هذه الصّومعة حتّى أخلوا
فيها وحدي وأفعل ما أريد وقالت ما هذا مكان
الّذي تريدان ولكن يطلع معي من أراد منكما
في الاول فركنا الى قولها فقالت لهما انا أطلع
اسبق [ص 39-ب] أعدل الموضع واُخلي بروحي
فقالا ### لها افعلي ما تري فقامت سوسنه
فطلعت إلى الصّومعة وأغلقت الباب وردمته
بالحجارة وطلعت لهما من على صومعتها وقالت
يا أعدآ الله والله لقد ذهبت عبادتكما باطلاً وقد
استحقّيتما النّار عبدتما الله تعالى سبعماِية سنة
وطلبتما تعصونه بعد ذلك أمضيا من عندي

فعليكما لعنة الله فمضيا من عندها وقد تأسّفا
عليها وكيف انفلتت منهما وتشاوروا على ما
يفعلا فقال هرم يا أخي ندخل المدينة ونسعى في
حديث الجارية إلى الملك فيحرقها بالنّار ونقول
انّها زنت ونسبق بالشّكوى فسارا جميعاً [ص 40-آ]
إلى أن دخلا المدينة فلمّا عاينوهم الناس أقبلوا
إليهما يسلّموا عليهما ويتبركوا بهما وقالوا لهما
ما الذي تريدان وما الذي أنزلكما من
صومعتكما فقالا حاجة عُرضت لنا عند الملك ثمّ
أقبلا إلى قصر الملك فدخلا إليه وسلّما عليه
فرفع قدرهما وترحّب بهما وقال ما الذي
أنزلكما من صومعتكما فقالوا ايها الملك ما
أنزلنا إلاّ انت أنت اسكنت عندنا امرأة زانية
وقد وضح عندنا وعاينّاها فلمّا صحّ عندنا اتينا

نُعلمك بها وعاينّاها وأبصرناها على غير حقيقة فقال لهما الملك قولكما عدل [ص 40-ب] صادق فأيّ قتلة تشتهياها نقتلها قالا تحرقها بالنّار فقال الملك أنا افعل ذلك في غداة إن شأ الله تعالى وخرجا من عنده ##### العبّاد وبات الملك قلقاً حزيناً على الجارية وقد تحيّر في أمره ما يدري ما يفعل فلمّا اصبح الصّباح ركب الملك فرسه العقاب وأمر أصحابه أن يخرجوا الحطب في رحبة واسعة ففعلوا ذلك ومضى الملك من ضيق صدره يتفرّج في الشجر والبستان فمرّ بروضة حسنة خضرة فنظر فيها نظرة فوجد فيها عين ما تجري فترل وشرب منها وغسل يديه ووجهه [ص 41-آ] فبينما هوكذلك إذ نظر إلى ستّة صبيان وعلى رؤسهم حطب ولا شكّ أنهم

عطشوا فقال الملك هؤلاء الصبيان قد جأوا تعابا
وإن أبصروني لم يريدوا المأ وأربح الخطييه والإثم
فقام من موضعه واستخبا خلف حايط خراب
وقال أريد أن أسمع ما يقولوا هؤلاء الصبيان
فأقبلوا فرموا الحزم الحطب عن رؤسهم وقلعوا
ثيابهم وسبحوا في المإ ثمّ طلعوا ولبسوا ثيابهم
وأخرجوا خبزاً كان معهم واكلوا فلمّا فرغوا
من اكلهم قال واحد من الصبيان يا إخوتي
قوموا بنا واسرعوا حتّى نحضر حرق سوسنه
بالنّار وكيف يحرقها الملك لأنّ هرم وهريم
العابدان [ص 41-ب] أبصروها وهي تزني وأقبلا
وشهدا عليها بما أبصرا فقال آخر من الصبيان
والله يا <ا>إخوتي ما يحملني قلبي أن انظر إلى
امرأة تقيّة نقيّة عابدة زاهدة تُحرق بالنّار فقالوا

له الصبيان العابدان شهدا عليها بالزنا قال والله
يا إخوتي انهما لكاذبان آثمان وتريدوا تبصروا
صحّة قولي قالوا نعم قال يكون الواحد منكم
هرم والآخر هريم ففعلوا ذلك فصاح بالصّبي
الواحد فأقبل إليه وبقي الآخر بعيد فقال له انت
رأيت سوسنه تزني قال نعم قال فمن زنا بها قال
رجل شابّ أسود اللّحية أدميّ اللّون تامّ القامه
حسن الخلقه قال له عُد إلى موضعك وصاح [ص
42-آ] <وصاح> بالآخر فأقبل اليه فقال له يا
هريم أنت رايت سوسنه تزني قال نعم قال صف
لي هذه الذي زنا بها قال غلام أجرد أمرد لا
نبات بعارضيه ابيض اللّون قصير ألقامه حسن
الخلقه فقال يا إخوتي كما اختلف قولكما
وكذبتما فكذلك يختلف قول هرم وهريم فلمّا

سمع الملك كلامهم خرج وفرح فرحاً شديداً وخرج إليهم فسلّم عليهم وقال للصبي يا ولدي تجي معي تقضي بين العابدين بهذا القضا فقال الصبي ايها الملك ما ترى حالتي وما انا فيه ليس أصلح ان اقضي بين النّاس فقال له الملك أنا افصّل لك ثياب وألبسك الزّينة والطّيلسان وتقضي بينهما فقال له أنا افعل [ص 42-ب] ذلك إن شأ الله تعالى ورجع الملك إلى المدينه وأمر النّاس أن يحضروا بالغد فلمّا اصبح الصّباح وأشرقت الشّمس بعث خلف الصبي وألبسه ثياب القضا وعمل على رأسه الزينة والطيلسان ونصب له كرسيّاً حسناً فاجلسه فوقه واجتمع رؤسآ اهل البلد والزهّاد والعبّاد فأمر الصبي باحضار هرم وهريم العابدان فأحضرا وجلسا

بين يديه فقال لهما الصبي يا هرم ويا هريم أنتما
نظرتما سوسنه تزني قالا نعم ونحنا عاينّا ذلك
مراراً فالتفت الصبي إلى الشهود وقال لهم شهدتم
على لفظهما قالوا نعم ثمّ أمر ان يفرّقوا بينهما
ففعلوا ذلك وجعلوا كلّ واحد ناحيةً ناحيةً دون
صاحبه ثمّ استدعى بهرم وحده [ص 43-آ] فقال له
يا هرم أنت رأيت هذه الجارية سوسنه زنت قال
نعم قال فمن الّذي زنا بها وأيش صفته قال غلام
أجرد أمرد لا نبات بعارضيه ابيض اللّون قصير
القامه حسن الخلقه قال وفي أيّ وقت رايتها قال
رأيتها عند الهاجره فما نزلت إلا عند غياب
الشّمس فقال الصبي ردّوه إلى موضعه فردوه إلى
موضعه وأمر باحضار هريم فوقف بين يديه فقال
له الصبي يا هريم قل ولا تقل إلاّ الحقّ قال نعم

قال انت تشهد على سوسنه العابدة انها بغت وزنت قال نعم قال رأيتَ ذلك بحقيقه# العيان قال نعم قال مع من زنت قال مع رجل أسود اللحية أدميّ اللّون [ص 43-ب] تامّ القامه قال في أيّ وقت رأيتها قال عند غياب الشّمس والإنصراف إلى انفجار الصّباح فقال له الصبي والله لقد كذبتما جميعاً وانّكما آثمان فقالوا النّاس ايها الملك أمر بقتلهما فقال الصبي يا قوم لا تعجلوا عليهما بالقتل فتريّحوهما بل أحرقوهما بالنّار كما اراد أن <ان> يفعلا بالجارية التّقية النّقية العابدة الزاهدة فأحضروهما جميعا وقرّروهما بما جرى منهما وأنّ الشيطان سوّل لهما ما فعلوه فلمّا سمعوا الناس منهما رجموهما بالحجارة وحملوهما بعد أن كتّفوهما بالحبال

وألقوهما في الحفيرة التي<ي> قد كانت حُفرت

من أجل سوسنه وردموهما بالحطب [ص 44-آ]

والنّار فلم يزال لهما كذلك حتّى احترقا وصارا

رماداً ثم التفت الملك إلى الصبي وقال له يا ولدي

من أبوك فقال زكريّا عليه السّلام فقال له الملك

صدقت هذه الثمرة من هذه الشّجرة ثم أخلع

على الصبي الخلع الحسنة وزوّجه بجارية حسنا

وانشدوا في المعنى شعر من يحتفر حفرة يوماً

يشين بها

فإن حَفَرتَ فَوسِّع حِينَ تَحتَفِرُ<وا>

إنَّ الشّبَابَ لَهُم عُذرٌ اذا جَهِلوُا

ولَيس يُقبَل مِن ذِي شيبة عذرُ<وا>

ثم انّه ركب من وقته وساعته ووُزرآيه وأهل

مملكته وجيوشه ودخل إلى الدّير الّذي فيه

سوسنه ودخل الى عند الجاريه فحدّثها بحديث هرم وهريم العابدان الذي كانا [ص 44-ب] في جوارها فكان جوابها للملك مَن لم يكفيه الله تعالى تعب ثمّ أنّ الملك ودّعها ورجع إلى المدينة ولم تزل الجاريه تعبد الله ## تعالى حتى اتاها اليقين فماتت فحزن الملك عليها حزناً طويلاً وكفّنها ودفنها إلى جانب أمّها ورمى الدنيا عن قلبه والتّاج عن رأسه والإكليل عن جبينه وسلّم المُلك لولده وطلع إلى الدّير الذي كانت فيه سوسنه <فيه> ساكنه ولم يزل يعبد الله عزّ وجلّ فيه حقّ عبادته حتّى أتاه اليقين فمات رحمه الله عليه

تمّ الحديث

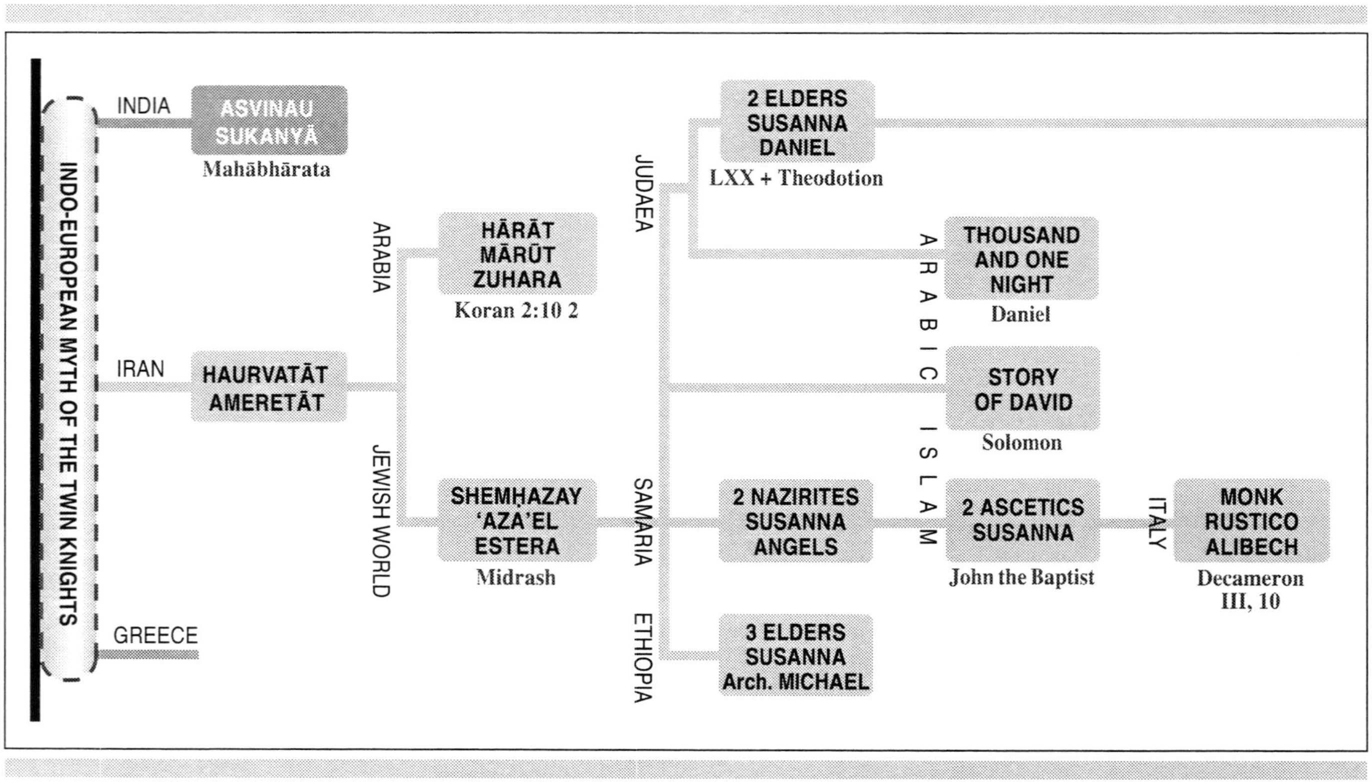

INDO-EUROPEAN MYTH OF THE TWIN KNIGHTS
INDIA
ASVINAU SUKANYĀ
Mahābhārata
IRAN
HAURVATĀT AMERETĀT
GREECE
ARABIA
HĀRĀT MĀRŪT ZUHARA
Koran 2:10 2
JEWISH WORLD
SHEMḤAZAY 'AZA'EL ESTERA
Midrash
JUDAEA
2 ELDERS SUSANNA DANIEL
LXX + Theodotion
SAMARIA
2 NAZIRITES SUSANNA ANGELS
ETHIOPIA
3 ELDERS SUSANNA Arch. MICHAEL
A R A B I C I S L A M
THOUSAND AND ONE NIGHT
Daniel
STORY OF DAVID
Solomon
2 ASCETICS SUSANNA
John the Baptist
ITALY
MONK RUSTICO ALIBECH
Decameron III, 10

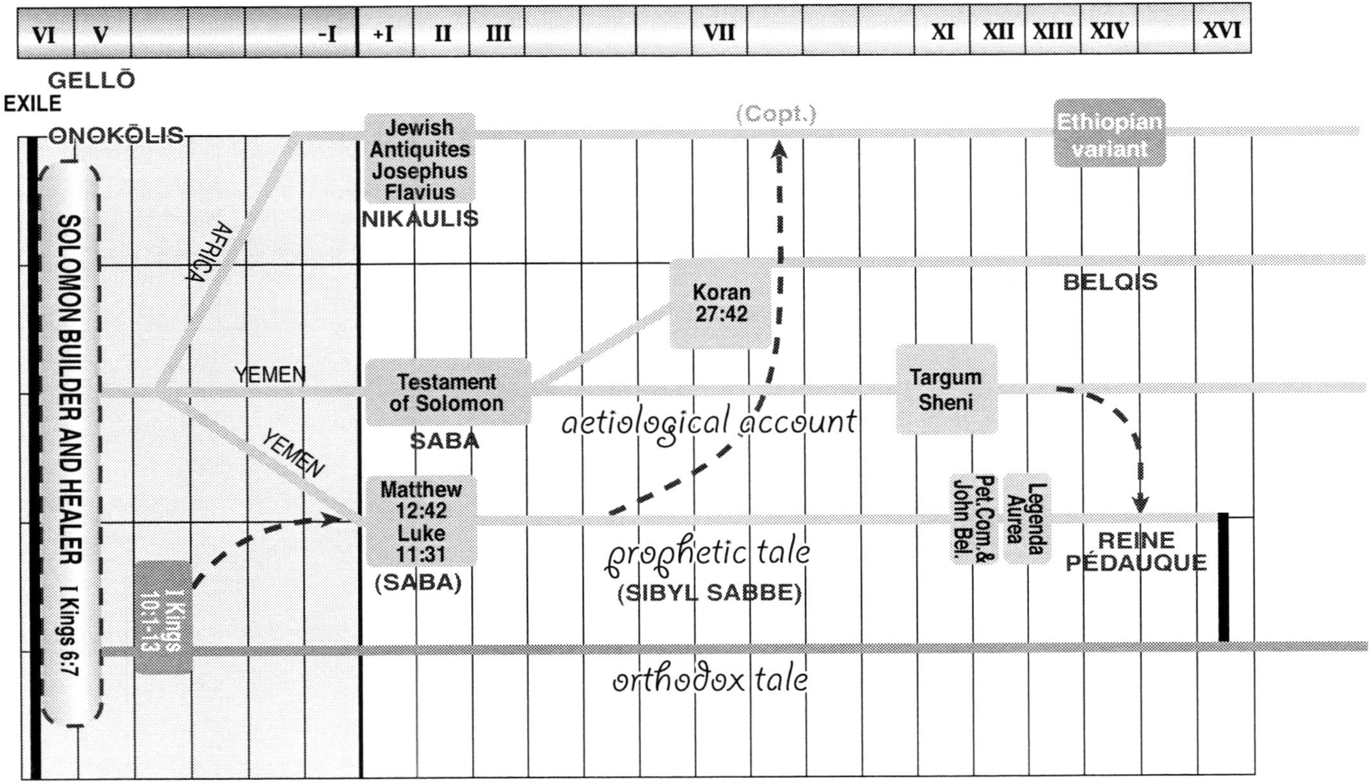
VI
V
-I
+I
II
III
VII
XI
XII
XIII
XIV
XVI
GELLŌ
EXILE
ONOKŌLIS
SOLOMON BUILDER AND HEALER
I Kings 6:7
AFRICA
YEMEN
YEMEN
I Kings 10:1-13
Jewish Antiquites Josephus Flavius
NIKAULIS
Testament of Solomon
SABA
Matthew 12:42 Luke 11:31
(SABA)
(Copt.)
Koran 27:42
aetiological account
prophetic tale
(SIBYL SABBE)
orthodox tale
Targum Sheni
Pet.Com.& John Bel.
Legenda Aurea
Ethiopian variant
BELQIS
REINE PÉDAUQUE